Desa Philadelphia

111 Shops
in Los Angeles
That You Must
Not Miss

Photographs by Lyudmila Zotova

emons:

For Aaron, who lets me feel like I've got it all figured out,
and Lilly, who reminds me that figuring it out is the fun part. – D.P.

© Emons Verlag GmbH
All rights reserved
Design: Eva Kraskes, based on a design
by Lübbeke | Naumann | Thoben
Edited by Katrina Fried
Maps: altancicek.design, www.altancicek.de
© Cover icons: iStockphoto.com / © StanRohrer,
iStockphoto.com / © Adjust, iStockphoto.com / © Brosa,
iStockphoto.com / © CoffeeAndMilk,
iStockphoto.com / © SteveCollender, iStockphoto.com / © DNY59
Printing and binding: Grafisches Centrum Cuno, Calbe
Printed in Germany 2015
ISBN 978-3-95451-615-5
First edition

Did you enjoy it? Do you want more?
Join us in uncovering new places around the world on:
www.111places.com

Foreword

Sand, surf, and the Hollywood sign are enduring symbols of Los Angeles. We do love our beaches and yes, we sometimes rub shoulders with a movie star or two while running errands or grabbing coffee. But there's so much more to our beautiful sprawling city. However you define it – by ethnicity, environment, or economics – L.A. is one of the most diverse places on the planet and Angelenos are extremely proud of their differences, as well as their contradictions.

For example, in addition to time spent lying on the sand, an L.A. weekend often includes a hike or, in our winter months, a trip up to snow-capped elevations in search of fresh powder. Natural water looms large in our culture, but domestic water is a scarce commodity. Our cuisine is called California fusion, but it is actually a mash-up of flavors and dishes indigenous to other parts of the globe. We live in our cars as much as we do our homes; have fashion tastes that range from red-carpet-ready to laid-back denim; and while we love a good trend (Uggs and shorts anyone?) we are also intent on expressing our individuality.

While it is impossible to highlight the full breadth of L.A.'s deeply seductive retail offerings in any one book, every shop profiled in these pages represents a quintessential local passion. If you live in Los Angeles, I hope you'll discover some new haunts that offer a different take on your particular brand of Southern California living. From the best surf shop in Santa Monica to Persian ice cream in Westwood, to custom-made wedding gowns in Downtown, and freshly milled grains in Pasadena, we've covered the city's best shopping hot spots. If you're only passing through, this unconventional mix of glamorous, quirky, fun, surprising, and always stylish stores will introduce you to an assortment of L.A. experiences. Chances are you'll even find a piece of wherever you call home among them.

111 Shops

1__25 Degrees
The hot spot for a perfect burger

The Hollywood Roosevelt Hotel is a quintessential Los Angeles hot spot, even during the off-again periods of its love affair with the starlet crowd. After all, it was founded by Hollywood insiders (Douglas Fairbanks, Mary Pickford, and Louis B. Mayer were among the original investors), played host to the inaugural Academy Awards ceremony in 1929, was the site of Marilyn Monroe's first magazine shoot (when she was still Norma Jean), and features artist David Hockney's million-dollar painted pool, so-called because a seven-figure appraisal convinced the California state legislature it should be exempt from a law requiring the bottoms of pools to be unadorned. Plus, it's named for President Teddy Roosevelt, the youngest person ever to hold the office.

It's also the home of 25 Degrees, a swanky burger bar located in the hotel's lobby and named after the difference in temperature between a raw patty and one that's well done (in Fahrenheit, of course). It's main burger offerings, named Number One, Two, and Three, are distinguished by the toppings that complement the juicy ground sirloin beef patty: caramelized onion / crescenza / bacon / arugula; roasted tomato / burrata / prosciutto / pesto; or green chili / chipotle / jack / avocado. There's also a yellowfin tuna patty, a veggie burger, or the option to build your own custom burger by choosing from among a cornucopia of extras. Tag on truffle fries and a Guinness milkshake (vanilla ice cream, chocolate sauce, and six ounces of stout) and you've got a premium version of the classic American meal.

The Roosevelt is located along the world-famous Hollywood Walk of Fame and 25 Degrees is open 24 hours, so on weekends after the clubs let out there can be a massive line. Lunch on a weekday is heavenly, with complimentary valet service and the ability to loiter a little before stepping back into the Hollywood glare.

Address 7000 Hollywood Boulevard, Los Angeles, CA 90028, +1 323.785.7244, www.25degreesrestaurant.com | Getting there US-101 to Highland Avenue/Hollywood Bowl. Valet parking. Or by public transit: Metro train Red Line to Hollywood and Highland Station. | Hours Open 24 hours

2 A+R

Extra-ordinary housewares

A+R is like your chicest girlfriend's "house ideas" Pinterest board come to life. This store has everything that you could want or need in order to furnish, decorate, and entertain. They carry chairs, tables, glassware, and all the little things that make a house a home: telephones, bathroom scales, clocks, and champagne buckets. The twist here is that every single item is designed so exquisitely that these everyday objects have been elevated from ordinary to extraordinary.

Go for seating and you'll be torn between Lucy chairs from Bend Goods, which are made from galvanized-iron wires welded together to create geometric shapes reminiscent of Art Nouveau sculptures like the Eiffel Tower; a puffed-up armchair from designer Jonas Wagell that was inspired by bread rising in a pan; and Oskar Zieta's Chippensteel 0.5 Chair, which looks like mylar balloons because it's made from chromed metal that has been inflated using high-pressure air. Glassware from Lee Broom consists of delicate lead crystal balanced on Italian marble and appropriately named "On the Rocks." A bathroom scale doubles as a wall hanging. And a champagne pail, reimagined for Maison Martin Margiela, resembles a stainless-steel industrial paint bucket.

The geniuses behind this concept store are (A)ndy Griffith plus (R)ose Apodaca, who are inspired by global approaches to modern design. They scour the earth for interesting takes on housewares and then import them to their two L.A. retail shops. The sales staff is equally enthusiastic about the products, and while well aware that the great design is what attracts buyers, is also eager to demonstrate how well these items function. You'll want to snatch up the store phone, an elegantly simple cordless masterpiece from Punkt with hands-free functions, cool ringtones, and the perfect modern aesthetic, which is cheekily called the "landline phone."

Address 171 S La Brea Avenue, Los Angeles, CA 90036, +1 323.692.0086,
www.aplusrstore.com, info@aplusrstore.com | **Getting there** I-10 to La Brea Avenue.
Parking behind store. | **Hours** Daily 11am–6pm

3 Aldik Home

Where Christmas lasts for months

At Aldik, the Christmas season officially launches on October 1st (there's an in-store party to kick things off). By then the store's employees have already spent two months transforming the 24,000-square-foot showroom into a winter wonderland. Soon after, interior decorators, set designers, and event planners start descending. October is a busy month for shooting Christmas-themed episodes of television shows, not to mention those ubiquitous commercials that try to lure shoppers in early. And this being Hollywood, exacting celebrity clients will soon be hosting large holiday bashes at their 90210 mansions.

The moment Richard Gold launched an artificial flowers business in 1951, Christmas decorations became his best sellers, so he kept expanding. Today Aldik offers a "Christmas tree lot" with dozens of twinkling, impeccably ornamented artificial trees. In the early years, Gold and his staff tried to keep customers from touching their masterpieces, until they realized people usually bought anything they were allowed to "pick" off the trees. These days, shoppers are encouraged to claim anything they find inspiring.

Aldik carries all the traditional trimmings associated with the season: sparkling ribbons, religious iconography, Santas, serene angels, and "snow-covered" wreaths and garlands. The trees supply the wow factor, as well as the ideas, so Aldik offers a wide variety of colors and sizes.

The rest of the year Aldik is known for silk flowers and plants that look impressively natural. There's even a "Custom Tree Bar" where customers can choose foliage for one-of-a-kind replicas of popular trees, like ficus, wisteria, or bougainvillea, that are made using actual tree branches to heighten the realism. The trees start at about $100 and can soar up to $800 depending on the size. But in perpetually drought-stricken California, a tree that won't die may be a good investment.

Address 7651 Sepulveda Boulevard, Van Nuys, CA 91405, +1 818.988.5970,
www.aldikhome.com | Getting there I-405 to Sherman Way or Roscoe Boulevard.
Parking lot. | Hours Mon–Sat 9am–6pm, Sun 11am–5pm

4 Allure Pharmacy

For a precisely personal prescription

Engaging a pharmacist at a chain drugstore often means waiting, then waiting some more, then dealing with someone who's less than helpful. Those who prefer a more personal touch will appreciate Allure Pharmacy. Located in tony Brentwood, Allure thrives on great customer service that extends all the way to what's in the bottles.

Allure specializes in compounding, where the pharmacist works with doctors to create personalized drugs, due to allergies, inability to swallow large pills, or for other reasons specific to each patient. It's a "made from scratch" method that's a throwback to the days before mass manufacturing when all pharmacists prepared medications rather than dispensed them. As drug companies grew, compounding declined. Now the practice is enjoying a resurgence, with pharmacists creating customized dosages, strengths, and even flavors of medications.

Allure's owner, and pharmacist, Dr. Ben Kadkhoda, worked in several pharmacies around Los Angeles – large chains and small family-owned businesses – where he gained experience with compounding. The growing popularity of the practice gave him the confidence to open his own pharmacy, even in a city where there's a CVS or Rite Aid on every corner.

Kadkhoda says the real reason people come back, however, is for the personal attention. He and his staff go above and beyond to provide quick and courteous service, even wrangling with insurance companies to straighten out approvals. Kadkhoda says there's also a misperception that large chains have better prices, but once customers realize that's not true, they favor the small-town treatment.

Allure also carries everything else you'll find at a regular drug store – cosmetics, greeting cards, toys, gifts, and the like. And they have a wide range of over-the-counter, nonprescription medications. So, even if all you need is some advice and a little TLC, they've got you covered.

Address 11670 San Vicente Boulevard, Los Angeles, CA 90049, +1 310.826.1111, www.allurepharmacyla.com, info@allurepharmacyla.com | Getting there I-405 to Wilshire Boulevard. Parking behind store or metered street parking. | Hours Mon–Fri 9am–7pm, Sat 10am–5pm

5__Apolis

Purposeful globe-trotting

The word *apolis* is Greek for a person without a city or country, which in modern context means someone who considers himself a global citizen. This is the guy Apolis caters to. He wears stylish but comfortable clothing, appreciates great quality but isn't a showoff, and most of all, cares about the world.

The shop is home to a line of apparel designed by Raan Parton, who started the business with his brother Shea. The clothes are a combination of the clean lines favored by Savile Row tailors and the soft, comfortable materials "lumbersexuals" seem drawn to. Many of their items are either manufactured by co-ops the Partons partner with in developing countries, or made in downtown L.A. Their indigo flannel button-down shirts, for example, are made by a 90-year-old Honduran tailoring cooperative using chambray-type wool milled in Japan. The store's signature tote bags ($28–$68) are hand-sewn by women in Bangladesh, then finished in L.A. with details like vegetable-tanned leather straps.

Apolis dresses its clients from head to toe. Other standout pieces include the chore jacket based on outerwear worn by blue-collar workers; the mason courier bag, an elegant but manly weekend bag; and an Italian leather military-style boot made by a 100-year-old family-owned factory in Portugal. The Parton brothers and their colleagues are the store's best models, dressing as the world's most stylish business travelers.

Apolis is located in downtown's Arts District, one of the city's recently trendy areas. It is surrounded by destination restaurants and stores like Poketo, which carries art-driven accessories; and Alchemy, a gallery, retail shop, and events space owned by Raan's wife, Lindsey. Apolis also hosts events, and members of the community are always welcome to come in for a cup of coffee. It's all part of being a good global citizen.

OUR STORY

In 2004, brothers Raan and Shea Parton founded Apolis with a simple idea that business can create social change. Their travels abroad immersed them in personal stories of struggle and survival and inspired them to create a business model that improves people's lives. Along with their commitment to global advocacy, they also understand the importance of sourcing and manufacturing locally. Whether it means partnering with manufacturers in Bangladesh, Peru, India, or around the corner in Los Angeles, the Partons have used their model of "advocacy through industry" to empower people to determine their own future.

LOS ANGELES
CALIFORNIA
USA

Address 806 E Third Street, Los Angeles, CA 90013, +1 855.894.1559, www.apolisglobal.com, service@apolisglobal.com | Getting there Take US-101 to Alameda Street, I-5 to Fourth Street, or I-10E to Alameda Street. Street parking. | Hours Mon–Wed 12pm–6pm, Thurs 12pm–7pm, Fri–Sat 11am–7pm, Sun 11am–6pm

6 _ Artful
A browser's paradise

Nancy Lombardi, the owner of Artful, likes to say there's a gift in her store for everyone, and a survey of the eclectic offerings seems to confirm this. The small shop is chock-full of handcrafted goods that make perfect birthday, thank-you, and anniversary presents.

Among the store's best sellers: hard-to-find decorative nail files made of glass (coveted by professional manicurists), and toddler and baby-sized rocker T-shirts featuring Madonna, Bowie, Dylan, and the Beatles. There are also cedar wood night-lights, duct-tape wallets, clocks, toys, paintings, books, lotions, scarves, calendars, perfumed oils, jewelry made of every material imaginable ... and more.

Another passion of Lombardi's is finding quality goods to sell at affordable price points. She carries $3 blessing rings by the Los Angeles-based husband-and-wife team of Whitney Howard Designs. The rings are actually coins made from recycled lead-free pewter and inscribed with emotion-inspiring words such as "Love," "Healing," "Bravery," and "Gratitude." They can be strung together to make bracelets or necklaces or simply slipped into a pocket.

Lotion from Chymia Hand & Body, based in South Salt Lake, Utah, is $6; a book of haiku about cats is $22; clocks made from ceramic tiles by artist Luis Sanchez are $40. Lombardi also posts bios of the artists she carries and it's cool to read about the inspiration for their creations.

Artful's jewelry, which perhaps offers the greatest variety in terms of both aesthetics and price, ranges from inexpensive collected vintage items to original designs from artists like Jivita Harris Casey, Grazyna Kiewicz, Jennifer Boyle, and Eric Casey that cost a few hundred dollars.

Lombardi is proud that the store has become such a browser's paradise, so she is frequently redecorating and moving things around to keep the shop and its merchandise looking fresh to repeat visitors.

7_Atomic Records
Still spinning the originals

Vinyl enthusiasts from around the world know they have a friend in Steve Alper. He won't let them travel for hours to reach his shop without guaranteeing something special. For the customer who collects live albums recorded at unusual venues (if there were an album of the Beatles' rooftop concert, Alper would be all over it), it's like having a personal record concierge who's always on the lookout.

There are thousands of used records on display at Atomic and each and every one has been hand chosen by Alper or his business partner. Alper never buys anything sight unseen, and now that his reputation precedes him, he usually gets the first call whenever a collection is being disbanded – like when someone working for the Maharishi offered up a stack of his holiness's records (there was nothing special, no limited-edition Beatles or Beach boys, mostly American jazz). The Smithsonian calls too; if they are looking for something particular for their collection, they know Alper may well have come across it.

It's not that Alper only stocks rare records, far from it. He's got vinyl of every genre, and you can score some albums for as little as 50 cents, although prices do vary quite a bit. He also carries CDs for 99 cents. But it's hard to find affordable records these days and the ones at Atomic, although secondhand, have to be in great condition to make the cut. Alper also cycles out merchandise every three days or so. The great stuff never lasts that long anyway. Plus he wants regulars to have a new experience every time they come in.

Alper grew up in Los Angeles working at and frequenting record shops. He opened Atomic in the 1990s – even as music retailers like Tower Records and Sam Goody were closing – because he wanted to preserve the record store experience: that wonderful act of wandering the aisles, flipping through album art, and walking out with one perfect find tucked underarm.

Address 3812 W Magnolia Boulevard, Burbank, CA 91505, +1 818.848.7090,
www.atomicrecordsla.com, atomicrecords@charter.net | Getting there US-101 to Lankershim
Boulevard–Universal City; SR 134 to Cahuenga Boulevard or Pass Avenue–Burbank.
Metered street parking. | Hours Mon–Sat 11am–7pm, Sun 12pm–5pm

8 Berlins

A Thai / German twist on boba

Angelenos love boba. Shops selling the Taiwanese bubble tea can be found all over the city, with lines as long as Starbucks'. Most of them sell the garden variety milk and fruit teas. A powder to make green jasmine tea frequently serves as the base ingredient with milk and fruit syrup added, and tapioca balls at the bottom. Some places also make instant boba, where they simply add water to a tea / milk / fruit powder.

Unexpectedly, one of the best places to find boba in Los Angeles is a Thai / German mashup café called Berlins. Nadia Khamthawee and Paul Korsakul, who came to Los Angeles from Thailand to learn to speak English, established the shop – originally called Boba Studio – infusing their own culture into their teas. It was successful enough that when they decided to move back to Thailand they were able to sell the business.

Enter brothers Simon and Matthias Classen. Simon and his family relocated to Los Angeles from Germany to work and fell in love with the lifestyle. He then convinced Matthias to make the move and start a business with him. They wanted to sell $8 German döner kebap, their country's most popular fast-food sandwich, and realized it might be easier to introduce döner to loyal boba customers instead of starting from scratch. They renamed the shop *Berlins* as a reminder of home, but assured the regular clientele that the Thai boba tea would remain on the menu.

Traditional Thai iced tea begins with a strong brew of Ceylon or black tea spiced with star anise or tamarind. Berlins' basic signature drink, Thai milk tea, is black tea with milk and boba, topped with fresh strawberries. Each drink is composed individually using all-natural, organic ingredients, beginning with freshly brewed green, black, or jasmine green tea. With prices for the drinks in the $3 to $4 range, it's a Taiwanese / Thai / German match made in boba heaven.

Address 8474 W Third Street, Los Angeles, CA 90048, +1 323.951.0847, www.eatberlins.com, info@eatberlins.com | **Getting there** I-10 to La Cienega Boulevard. Free parking lot. | **Hours** Daily 11:30am–8pm

9__ Big Kid
For the child in all of us

Imagine a 1950s style drive-up restaurant with changing themes, such as space exploration, Hawaiian luaus, and cowboys and Indians. Plus, right in the middle there's a store featuring the most popular toys of the era. Sounds awesome, doesn't it? David Levy thought so. The former magazine publisher spent a great deal of time trying to find the perfect location for his retail vision, but came up empty-handed.

Then a unique opportunity presented itself. A storefront became available in a strip mall in Sherman Oaks, right next door to Nat's Early Bite, a bustling retro diner with loyal customers who come from all across the southland for a hearty, no-frills, all-day breakfast. Levy convinced the owners at Nat's to connect Big Kid to their paging system and to suggest that patrons hang out in the shop while they wait for their table.

A visit to Big Kid is like stepping back in time. The center of the store is set up like a living room brimming with toys and games and featuring an old black-and-white television set that's always on, playing shows from yesteryear such as *Casper the Friendly Ghost* and *Lassie*. The rest of the shop is stocked with new and vintage products, all aimed at celebrating baby boom childhoods: superhero figurines and lunchboxes, original Barbies, Little Golden Books (including the recent best seller *Everything I Need to Know I Learned from a Little Golden Book*), and DVDs of classic TV series. It's a pleasant surprise to discover a line of replica Pan Am travel bags, priced from about $60. There are also Shrinky Dinks, an assortment of candies, and an antique soda-pop machine that still dispenses Brownie Caramel Root Beer, Frostie Blue Cream Soda, Nesbitt's Orange, Lemmy Lemonade, and Bubble Up.

The only drawback is that sometimes word comes from Nat's before you're ready to put the toys down. That's okay, says Levy, people always come back.

Address 14109 Burbank Boulevard, Sherman Oaks, CA 91401, +1 818.785.9208, www.bigkidcollectibles.com, info@bigkidcollectibles.com | Getting there I-405 to Burbank Boulevard. US-101 to Woodman Avenue. Parking lot. | Hours Tues–Fri 10am–6pm, Sat 9am–6pm, Sun 9am–4pm

10__Black & White Car Rental

This is how we roll

It's difficult to get around Los Angeles without a car. Buses between the county's various municipalities aren't always in sync; the light rail system doesn't cover the entire city; and places are far too spread out to make walking a pleasant or realistic option. Yes, getting around this town calls for a set of wheels. And if you need to rent a ride, why not take the opportunity to experience something truly special?

Go for a luxury car rental at Black & White and roll like royalty, which in L.A. means you'll feel like an A-lister. Here's what possible: a Rolls Royce Drophead Coupe, a Maserati Gran Turismo, a Ferrari 458 Spider, or, if you're environmentally conscious, a Tesla Model S.

But you need to have some serious disposable cash to go for cars like these. A Bentley Flying Spur costs more than $1,700 a day to rent, and a Lamborghini Aventador Roadster goes for upwards of $4,900. A Tesla almost starts to feel like a bargain at a daily rate of $650.

Angelenos are used to tricked-out cars. We see exotics around town all the time, and even in the most modest neighborhoods, it's not unusual to spot a high-performance vehicle parked in a driveway. Tax loopholes are kind to people who lease vehicles as business expenses, and if you're going to write off a car, it might as well be a Beamer, an Audi, or a Benz, don't you think?

Those kinds of cars are available at Black & White too, and for significantly less than the exotics. An Audi A3 convertible or a Mercedes CLA 250 can be had for less than $150 a day. And if you'd rather keep it really low key, Black & White also has standard cars from the likes of Mitsubishi, Volkswagen, or Chevrolet.

If you can only afford to splurge just a teeny bit, consider the car that has become the standard in Los Angeles, driven by celebs, hipsters, and ordinary grandpas alike: the Toyota Prius hybrid.

Address 8800 Burton Way, Beverly Hills, CA 90211, +1 310.274.1144, www.bwrentacar.com, info@bwrac.com | **Getting there** I-10 to Robertson. Free parking. | **Hours** Mon–Fri 7:30am–9pm, Sat–Sun 8am–6pm

11 BlueCollar Working Dog

Catering to the professional canine

In a town where pooches of ever-shrinking sizes are toted around like fashion accessories, it's easy to forget that many of man's best friends have to work for their supper. Police and military dogs, search and rescue dogs, service and therapy dogs, competition dogs, and, of course (in a showbiz town), performing dogs, all clock in for duty. BlueCollar Working Dog is the first brick-and-mortar store dedicated to the needs of the hardest-working hounds in L.A.

Owners of "professional" dogs seldom get the kind of attention and service that is showered on the pampered-pet crowd, and BlueCollar has stepped in to fill the niche. The store stocks all the gear that working pups and their handlers use – equipment vests, whistles, backpacks, harnesses, clatter sticks, bite sleeves, and muzzles. It also carries several high-quality dog food brands and sells refrigerated meat for raw feeding, a practice that is growing in popularity among pet owners.

BlueCollar is the brainchild of Barry Hewitt, a trainer who specializes in working breeds. A former marine, Hewitt clearly has great respect for the career K-9 and their evolving jobs and roles. Breakthroughs in medical research, for example, have led to dogs being used for scent work in detecting Alzheimer's, various cancers, and other diseases. Still, Hewitt wants BlueCollar to be equally as welcoming to the family pet, and it's common to see dogs of all stations in its aisles.

It's not all work and no play at BlueCollar. The store sells lots of toys and treats. Hewitt trains dogs for canine competitions: those obstacle course extravaganzas that take over local parks on the weekends and, on the more professional level, even get television time. So he also provides the jumps, tunnels, and frisbees needed to put on a show. And of course there are some spoiling essentials too. After all, even working dogs should have their (spa) day.

Address 1533 Echo Park Avenue, Los Angeles, CA 90026, +1 213.977.9042,
www.bluecollarworkingdog.com | Getting there US-101 to Echo Park Avenue.
Street parking. | Hours Mon–Fri 9am–9pm, Sat 9am–8pm, Sun 10am–6pm

12_ Books and Cookies
A hangout for the toddler set

Of course, Books and Cookies sells books. They stock the superstars of contemporary toddler literature. Authors like Mo Willems, Eric Carle, Laura Numeroff, Ian Falconer, and others of their ilk are all in attendance. Their shop space, aka the Interactive Reading Room, is designed with comfortable seating to encourage in-store perusing, and your kids won't get the eye if they start clamoring to pull things off the shelves.

And of course they also sell cookies and plenty of yummy baked-good snacks. But Books and Cookies offers far more than the name implies. If the local coffee shop is where Mom and Dad like to escape to unwind, this is where their toddler wants to go to let off some steam. Particularly in the store's covered outdoor Learn & Play area, a stunning yard that's perfect for mellowing out but is really designed for active play, with a teepee, building blocks, dress-up area, Saturday-morning concerts, and a CedarWorks playset. Kids can check in for $7 and stay as long as they want (yes, a caregiver has to be in attendance, but it's a contained space so you can let a kid be a kid without fear of them wandering off). A third room, dubbed the Enrichment Center, is the setting for story time, music, and movement classes with highly qualified teachers.

That's another thing. Books and Cookies is designed and staffed by professionals trained in early-childhood education. The least experienced salespeople and assistants are likely to be local college students who are studying to be educators. The store is the brainchild of former teacher Chudney Ross, who is from a prominent showbiz family – her mother is music legend Diana Ross and three of her four siblings also are well-known performers. Chudney dabbled in modeling but after graduating from college signed up for a stint with Teach For America and found her calling. She's since published a highly-rated children's book, *Lone Bean*.

Address 2309 Main Street, Santa Monica, CA 90405, +1 310.452.1301, www.booksandcookiesla.com, info@booksandcookiesla.com | Getting there I-10W to Fourth Street. Metered parking. Or by public transit: Santa Monica Big Blue Bus Route 1 to Hollister Avenue. | Hours Mon–Sat 9am–5pm

13 Broken Horn Saddlery

Keeping the West western

Yes, there are still cowboys in California. Cowgirls too. And while urban sprawl has seriously threatened their lifestyles, dressage enthusiasts, Mexican-American vaqueros, and casual riders continue the traditions that gave the West its enduring personality. Even more surprising is that the largest shop in the West that caters to their needs is less than twenty miles from downtown L.A. Broken Horn Saddlery, a sprawling superstore with its own on-site factory, specializes in all the accouterments and equipment that a horse lover needs to happily roam Los Angeles's trails and roads.

Charlie and Mattie Nuzzo, who founded the business in 1956, started out making stable drapes before expanding into tack, with their store becoming well known in equestrian circles for its show saddles. Today, Broken Horn still employs master craftsmen who make and repair custom saddles as well as belt buckles, blankets, and other handmade products. Many of the store's craftsmen learned their trade from their fathers and grandfathers, continuing an art form that would otherwise disappear.

While this is an important supply depot for L.A.'s serious horse folk, Broken Horn also welcomes interlopers who might simply appreciate the fashion or wish to display an elaborate saddle as sculpture. For an authentic equestrian look that costs less than designer label imitations, you can pick up a nice pair of breeches and riding boots here. Or if it's a cowboy outfit you're after, staffers will fit and crease your hat or help you find the perfect pair of leather boots, available in sizes for children and adults and in a variety of colors (hot pink anyone?).

Though horse-keeping may continue to diminish in Los Angeles as urban development takes precedence over stables and open trails, the city remains a fiercely proud inheritor of its equine-loving Western heritage.

Address 1022 Leorita Street, Baldwin Park, CA 91706, +1 626.337.4088, www.brokenhornsaddlery.com, saddlery@earthlink.net | Getting there I-10 to Baldwin Park. Parking lot. | Hours Wed–Sat 10am–6pm, Sun 10am–5pm

14_ Broome Street General Store

7-Eleven meets Neiman Marcus

Broome Street General Store, owned by husband-and-wife team Sophie Esteban and Peter Graham, is named after Sophie's old street in New York City's West Village, where she had her first grown-up apartment. Back then, she stocked her place with all the things that represented adulthood – elevated versions of what you'd find at a home-goods emporium or corner market.

That early experience in domesticity inspired Esteban and Graham's general store concept. Located in a 1906 cottage that boasts a generous patio, Broome Street carries everything young sophisticated Angelenos would want in their homes. Niche brands like Coyuchi, Nuxe, Brooke Corson, and Le Petit Bateau can be found in the relevant "departments": housewares, apothecary, jewelry, and kids. There's a long counter nestled along one wall, behind which baristas serve up coffee from New York roaster Gimme!, as well as sandwiches, salads, and treats. The atmosphere feels less like you're in the middle of the city and more like you're on a road trip and just happen to discover the chicest little shop in town. The Grahams, who describe Broome Street as a "luxury convenience store," like to joke that their business is what the lovechild of 7-Eleven and Neiman Marcus would look like.

The espresso bar is a major draw and it's lovely to sit out in the front yard with a latte. Although people may come for the coffee, they leave with the goods. The store has become an oasis for the hipsters who live in the neighborhood. It's a one-stop shopping outpost they can walk to instead of having to drive to a variety of luxury boutiques.

The Grahams have also opened a sister store across the street that sells some clothing and furniture but mostly stocks high-end kitchenware – the type of supplies you need when you've moved past your singleton life and started raising a family.

Address 2912 Rowena Avenue, Los Angeles, CA 90039, +1 323.570.0405, www.broomestgeneral.com, sup@broomestgeneral.com | Getting there I-5 to Glendale Boulevard. Street Parking. | Hours Mon–Sat 8am–7pm, Sun 9am–5pm

15 _ Café de Leche

A neighborhood's signature beverage

Highland Park has recently become a destination for artist types looking for affordable rents and Craftsman fixer-uppers. It's also popular with young families, who've been priced out of nearby Silver Lake and Echo Park and like its proximity to downtown L.A. and Pasadena. Predominantly Latino since the 1970s, the neighborhood suffered through waves of gang violence before a turnaround in the mid-aughts. During that time its main claim to fame was that Quentin Tarantino shot *Reservoir Dogs* there.

Café de Leche captures the old and the new, with its emphasis on honoring the area's Latin flavor while offering the third-wave coffee culture of more affluent communities. It is owned by longtime Highland Park residents Anya and Matt Schodorf. Anya moved to L.A. from Nicaragua as a teenager; Matt is from the Midwest. They have become recognizable faces around their neighborhood, and frequently and earnestly stress that they are not gentrifiers.

Horchata con espresso, their signature beverage, is genuinely, and ingeniously, symbolic of Highland Park. The ingredients in horchata differ among Spanish-speaking countries, but most recipes call for milked seeds, nuts, or grain, to which sugar and cinnamon are added. Because of increased allergy awareness, most L.A. horchatas are now rice-based (nut-free, dairy-free, and gluten-free) and that's the case here. To this already delicious old-school concoction, Café de Leche adds espresso made from coffee sourced by Stumptown, the Portland-based roaster known for buying the highest quality beans from producers around the world.

Other highlights on the coffee menu include a Mexi Mocha (Mexican mocha) with cinnamon and allspice, an agave latte, and a mate latte. They also serve chai and assorted other teas.

Business is brisk, especially on the weekends, but it's always worth the wait.

Address 5000 York Boulevard, Los Angeles, CA 90042, +1 626.337.4088,
www.cafedeleche.net, info@cafedeleche.net | **Getting there** SR 110N to Avenue 52,
Highland Park. Metered street parking. | **Hours** Sun–Thurs 7am–6pm, Fri–Sat 7am–7pm

16 California Surplus Mart
Supplies for camping, emergencies, or a zombie attack

California Surplus Mart is located in a gritty part of Hollywood filled with small, black-box theaters (where actors keep their "instruments" tuned while waiting for their big break), no-frills low-income apartments, and young homeless people panhandling on the street. The store's bright yellow facade, covered with logos and product descriptions, makes California Surplus Mart a standout. But its striking exterior is nothing compared to the offerings inside. This emporium appears to have everything you could possibly need to survive in the woods – or fight off a zombie invasion. There are compasses, binoculars, scopes, and searchlights; gas masks, MREs (the ready-to-eat meals that troops depend on in the field), and flasks; parachutes, stun guns, batons, and much more.

Every city seems to have a store like this, the kind that appears to cater to believers of an impending apocalypse. But L.A. is earthquake territory, and many supplies sold here are actually needed for emergency preparedness. They are also the necessities for enjoying the great outdoors, which locals embrace enthusiastically. After all, within a few hours, you could be camping in the mountains of Angeles National Forest, hiking the deserts of Joshua Tree, or bird-watching along the lush riverbanks of McGrath State Beach.

The store also has a large selection of camouflage clothing, dog tags, and other military paraphernalia. There's a wide variety of workmen's wear from brands like Dickies, Carhartt, and Wrangler, as well as steel-toe boots, military-issue pea coats, backpacks, and hats, which get snapped up as fashion accessories.

Plus there are the types of items that you've always wondered where people find them – for example, the cheap, three-hole face masks popular with bank robbers on television shows, and those big jagged-edged knives that seem highly impractical for most non-nefarious tasks.

17 __ Camille, Rue de Mimo, & Marz

A happy threesome

Bohemian chic first came to South Pasadena in the 1970s, in the form of a store called Sonny's, which featured ethnic fashions from around the world. Three young women – Marcia Ellinger, Mimo Boghossian, and Camille DePedrini – were working there when Sonny's went out of business in the late '90s. Together they took over the lease, but each ran her own individual shop out of the single storefront. As their businesses grew, they took over three adjacent retail spaces and promptly cut doorways in their walls, reuniting as Camille, Rue de Mimo, and Marz.

The three stores now happily share real estate, great friendships, and loyal customers, but that's about where the similarities end. Marz, owned by Ellinger, is all about offering elevated everyday gifts. So the cards, books, toys, and household staples Marz sells are chock-full of personality and, frequently, humor. Boghossian and her sister Paulette Ledyard stock Rue de Mimo with whimsical global fashions from designers like Skunkfunk (dresses from Spain), Poetic License (shoes from England), and Ayala Bar (jewelry from Israel), much of which could best be described as wearable art. Camille offers special-occasion dresses, shoes, and bridal wear. DePedrini is an expert at creating modern styles inspired by vintage silhouettes, as demonstrated by her house line, which is complemented by clothing and accessories from like-minded labels.

The experience of shopping here is akin to wandering through a highly curated department store, with each section inspiring a different mood and different reasons to spend. The shops are located on Mission Street, South Pasadena's chic main drag. It's a hotbed of independent businesses: one-of-a-kind restaurants, galleries, and boutiques. All the owners know and patronize one another. It's like small-town America on the outskirts of L.A.

Address 1512–1516 Mission Street, South Pasadena, CA 91030; Camille: +1 626.441.7868, www.camilledepedrini.com, camilledepedrini@att.net; Rue de Mimo: +1 626.441.2690, www.ruedemimo.com, ruedemimo@gmail.com; Marz: +1 626.799.4032, www.marzgifts.com | Getting there SR 110N to South Orange Grove Boulevard. Metered street parking. | Hours Tues–Sat 11am–7pm, Sun 12pm–5pm

18 Centerfold International News

Keeping print alive

The Internet's devastating effect on the newsprint business has, sadly, forced many vendors to shut down, making the neighborhood newsstand largely a thing of the past. Luckily, there are still a few scattered around the city, and Centerfold International News is the oldest and best among them. A small blue shack adorned with *New York Times* and lottery logos, it has occupied a spot in West Hollywood for more than 40 years.

The stand is owned by Manuel Portillo, who bought it in 2006, and runs it with help from his brother Rene. The two have worked in the business for three decades, and although they've witnessed the decline of print firsthand, they're determined to stay open for all those who still love the smell of a freshly inked glossy magazine and the irreplaceable rustle of a newspaper.

Their newsstand is a browser's paradise but the brothers don't mind the loiterers. At Centerfold, it's still possible to discover a niche publication you've never heard of, and all sorts of interests are represented. The fashion magazines rule the roost, occupying prominent real estate near the cash register. This section of the city is a fashionista's paradise and stylish young women often pop in to get a double fix: nicotine and *Vogue*. The weeklies – from *Time* to *Us* – are also front-row mainstays. The aisles are filled with publications from around the world, both well known and obscure. Music lovers can geek out on *Mojo* and *Q*, tattoo enthusiasts may dig into *Inked* and *Tattoo Life*, and for style mavens, there's *Dolce* and *New African Woman*. As the store is named Centerfold, it's no surprise you'll also find a healthy selection of adult-themed magazines.

Customers seeking foreign-language newspapers will have less luck. Those are now the domain of the World Wide Web.

Address 716 N Fairfax Avenue, Los Angeles, CA 90046, +1 323.651.4822,
www.newstandinc.com, centerfoldinc1@gmail.com | Getting there I-10 to Fairfax
Avenue. Metered street parking. | Hours Mon–Sat 6am–11pm, Sun 6am–10pm

19_ ChocoVivo

From bean to bar

After quitting her CPA job, Patricia Tsai went on a culinary tour to Oaxaca, Mexico, for some recovery R & R. Given that the focus of the trip was on the cuisine of the region, which is known for its variety of moles, Tsai was mesmerized by just how much the locals enjoyed chocolate. "Their daily ritual was having a piece of chocolate," she says. "They ate it the way we drink coffee."

What Tsai also found striking was that the chocolate in Oaxaca wasn't the shiny, finished bars Americans are used to. "In Mexico it is very rustic. And it has texture and a whitish color to it," she adds. Tsai was so inspired, in fact, that she decided to become a chocolate maker.

After 10 long years of study (she had to return to corporate America to support her quest) Tsai opened ChocoVivo, where she makes bars the way Mayans and Aztecs did more than 2000 years ago – by stone grinding whole beans. She buys cacao directly from the man who has become her mentor, a farmer in Tabasco, Mexico, and makes only dark-chocolate products, never adding milk powder, soy lecithin, or any of the dozen or so other ingredients that usually crowd up the label of a typical candy bar.

ChocoVivo offers pure and blended chocolates, including a 100 percent cacao bar that provides enough of a kick to replace your daily joe. Tsai also mixes chocolate with whole-food ingredients like vanilla, hazelnut, sea salt, and peppercorns. Her Shangri-La bar includes toasted black sesame and chewy bits of goji berry. She does custom grinds for special events and large orders, as well.

Because the chocolate experience at ChocoVivo is so different (at least to the L.A. market), Tsai also considers herself an educator. She has even given a Ted Talk on her journey. Her passion for the ancient technique of chocolate making is relentless. "People say I must have been Mayan in my past life," she says. "Which is probably true."

Address 12469 Washington Boulevard, Culver City, CA 90066, +1 310.845.6259, www.chocovivo.com, info@chocovivo.com | **Getting there** I-405 to Culver Boulevard, Washington Boulevard. Metered street parking. | **Hours** Mon–Thurs 11am–9pm, Fri–Sat 9am–11pm, Sun 9am–9pm

20__ Church

Preaching the gospel of avant-garde

Church is tucked away inside a warehouse that seems to disappear under a cloud of gorgeous bright-green ivy. You may just walk on by, thinking it's the world's most exuberant hedge. But please find the entrance and ring the bell, because what's inside is revelatory.

Church is dedicated to avant-garde fashion, art, and home accessories. It's a cavernous space that feels like it could be the lair of Batman's smarter, cooler artist brother. Owned by Rodney Burns and David Malvaney, two longtime stylists who have worked for the best high-end boutiques and have the A-list clientele to prove it, Church caters to customers who are meticulous about what they wear.

To pull off these kinds of clothes, you've got to have some confidence. Church is the only store in the United States where you can find cutting-edge labels like B*+S, which is popular with celebrities like Lenny Kravitz, Halle Berry, and Steven Tyler; and India Flint, an Australian designer who uses natural plant dyes to create incredible prints.

The decor, which is also for sale, includes artwork from RETNA, a graffiti artist with a celebrity following known for his billboards and graphic murals around L.A.; and sculptor Mattia Biagi, whose Black Tar Mickey Mouse Candelabra goes for $25,000.

The truth is that Church is geared to those who can afford a $25,000 sculpture. Stylists come here to deck out clients for their paparazzi close-ups, red-carpet obligations, or music video shoots. Vintage lace gowns that could go from the Oscars to a rave run up to $11,000. The cheapest items are the basic tees, which start at around $120.

If you can afford the wares, you won't be disappointed. Same goes if you can't. The staff is incredibly friendly, and Burns and Mulvaney preach avant-garde for the masses. It's okay with them if some members of the congregation are just there to worship the artists.

Address 7277 Santa Monica Boulevard, West Hollywood, CA 90046, +1 323.876.8887, www.churchboutique.com, info@churchboutique.com | Getting there US-101 to Santa Monica Boulevard. Street parking. | Hours Mon–Sat 10:30am–6pm

21 __ Clockwork Couture
Ode to local time travel

Clockwork Couture didn't intend to be an outlet for *Doctor Who* merchandise. Owner Donna Ricci just thought it would be cool to erect a replica of the Doctor's TARDIS (his time travel vessel that's basically a blue phone booth) outside the shop's front door. But then the insatiable fans of the BBC's global hit series started showing up to find out what was to be had inside. And they weren't just satisfied with bow ties (although, as the eleventh Doctor Who would say, "Bow ties are cool"). So Clockwork Couture now has a room that features clothing, accessories, and artwork inspired by the show.

A Los Angeles native, Ricci was a goth girl who grew up to own an agency representing goth-girl models – tattooed, pierced, bespoked in black. But as she grew older, Ricci began longing for just a little more color in her life. That's when she discovered steampunk – the sub-genre of science fiction that draws on a mashup of Victorian / Edwardian and turn-of-the-century imagery – and the fashions it has inspired. While *Doctor Who* is not explicitly a steampunk show, its focus on time travel and its very British sensibility echo aspects of the genre.

Clockwork Couture's eponymous line for women features bustled skirts, interesting bits of hardware that buckle and snap, boots with buttons, and – in a nook called Victorian Secret ("We're waiting for that lawsuit," jokes Ricci) – corsets, garters, and other undergarments. For men, there are three-piece suits, pocket watches, and cuff links. There's even an on-staff milliner, as well as a corset maker.

The store also sells art by Disney illustrator Brian Kesinger. His silhouettes of all the actors who have played Doctor Who is a fan favorite, as are the bags of hand-blended teas with names like Chalmun's Canteana (that's one for *Star Wars* buffs). Time travelers appreciate a good "cuppa" and Clockwork Couture is all about providing everything they could possibly need.

Address 707 S Main Street, Burbank, CA 91506, +1 818.478.1515,
www.clockworkcouture.com | Getting there I-5 to Alameda, SR 134 to Bob Hope Drive.
Street parking. | Hours Mon, Wed, Thurs, Fri 10am–4pm, Sat 12pm–6pm, Sun 12pm–4pm

22 Crafted at the Port of Los Angeles

Meet the artisans

If Etsy, the online bazaar for handcrafted wares, came to life, Crafted is what it would look like. This market for artisan goods occupies a converted 1940s warehouse along the waterfront of the port of Los Angeles, where all manner of merchandise from around the world is unloaded from ships, placed on trucks, and sent off to permeate Southern California and cities across the country. Amidst all this, Crafted is like an ironic island of local ingenuity; a sea of booths stocked with handmade products from clothing to toys to art to housewares to plant arrangements, all manned by the artists themselves.

Crafted was inspired by Bergamot Station, the conglomerate of independent galleries in Santa Monica. But while Bergamot caters to luxury tastes and deep pockets, Crafted is welcoming to families of all economic brackets. They come to shop for unique items, watch DIY demonstrations, and learn how to make objects and products themselves. It feels like an updated version of what "family time" might have been like before Disneyland. A Belgian-inspired brewery and a fast casual restaurant are setting up in the warehouse next door and the courtyard between them is used for live bands and other pop-up events.

The waterfront itself is a hub of activity, with cruise-ship passengers on their way to or from distant locales. Less than two miles from the Crafted warehouse is the Battleship USS Iowa Museum, where visitors of all ages may tour the only battleship exhibit on the West Coast. USS *Iowa* was commissioned in 1940 during the presidency of Franklin D. Roosevelt and served for more than 50 years. In addition to learning about its heroic activities, visitors can see the special bathtub that was installed for Roosevelt to use during his trip to the Tehran Conference, the World War II strategy meeting with British Prime Minister Winston Churchill and Soviet Premier Joseph Stalin.

Address 112 E 22nd Street, San Pedro, CA 90731, +1 310.732.1270, www.craftedportla.com, info@craftedportla.com | Getting there I-110 to Harbor Boulevard. Parking lot. | Hours Fri–Sun 11am–6pm

23_Danny's Warehouse

Swan Lake essentials for less than a ten-spot

As soon as L.A. toddlers start taking movement classes, their moms begin to hear whisperings about a store that sounds like a secret club: Danny's Warehouse. Danny's sells all-new dance, gymnastics, and figure-skating apparel, shoes, and accessories by well-known brands for $10 or less.

Owner Danny Kessler's grandfather and father were in the discount clothing business long before Ross, Marshall's, and T.J.Maxx were neighborhood fixtures. Kessler grew up helping out in his dad's store, putting tags on clothes or sorting them for the racks. After failing at the discount fashion business himself (the corporate stores had a foothold by then), Kessler had a brainstorm: Why not apply what he knew about buying bulk clothing to active wear? Companies like Danskin, Capezio and Danshuz, happy to have a reliable means of clearing out old stock, began sending him boxfuls of products.

As an amateur gymnast, Kessler knew small dance and gymnastics studios across the country were always looking for deals. So, armed with the Yellow Pages and a $10 price point, he began cold-calling potential customers and the business took off. He went on to open a retail outpost, and 20 years later, brands that traditionally sell for $50 or more can still be found at Danny's for a bargain: $10 or $5 for leotards, dresses, costumes, and shoes; $3 for tights. The bulk warehouse atmosphere of the store is also unchanged and to the untrained eye it looks like a huge disorganized mess. Gigantic overflowing cardboard boxes contain apparel of the same color, regardless of style. And finding the right size usually requires some digging, especially in the $1 clearance bins, which are always filled with surprising finds.

But you won't notice anyone complaining. On a typical day at Danny's, you'll find moms, gymnasts, and club kids happily rummaging side by side, elbow deep in discount dancewear heaven.

24__dean.

Vintage sensibility, modern edge

Danny Dean Davis had planned to be a sociologist, but after graduating from UCLA in 1993 he took a position at a still relatively unknown company called Urban Outfitters, a retailer that was bucking the trend of mass-produced fashion, instead buying from smaller designers and artisans. Davis's job going from city to city to design new stores tickled his creative bone. So when he couldn't find "a wide leather watchband with a vintage feel," he made one himself. Then, when people began asking where he got it, he started custom designing. And when he roughed out a bag that also attracted attention, he decided to launch his business.

Between books and instructionals by other artisans (this was pre-YouTube tutorials), Davis learned how to create a line of accessories that filled what he saw as a gap in the market: "The craft had gone out of everything," he explains. In 1999, Davis established dean., opening the Silver Lake store in 2004, just as the authentically hip neighborhood was booming. He took aim at status bags, many of which he felt were "expensive but weren't well crafted."

A dean. bag harkens back to those Davis saw in 1970s leather shops – classic shapes, made distinctive with hand-applied details. He describes them as having "a vintage sensibility with a modern edge." Popular styles include the B 35, a zippered tote with studded short handles, and the B 09R, a teardrop-shaped bag made from reclaimed leather jackets.

Davis might not have become a sociologist but his business clearly benefits from his training. He gave the shop his middle name for its familiarity, simplicity, and cultural symbolism (think James Dean and Dean Martin). And choosing to identify his signature products by a number is definitely a statement. The UB 07 is the perfect choice for a weekend getaway, while the B 30 is all the bag you'll need for a night out on the town.

Address 3918 W Sunset Boulevard, Los Angeles, CA 90026, +1 323.665.2766, www.deanaccessories.com, danny@deanaccessories.com | Getting there US-101 to Silver Lake Boulevard. Metered street parking | Hours Daily 11am–7pm

25 Des Kohan

Dress like an insider

Desiree Kohan literally learned the fashion business from the street up. As a trend spotter for Gucci, Prada, and Miu Miu, the Angeleno scoured the streets of Europe for trends and shopped vintage stores to see what styles were still resonating. She then launched her own line, which was carried in Neiman Marcus, Saks, and Barneys, before opening a brick-and-mortar store and essentially cementing her reputation as a fashion goddess – someone who excels at everything from design to manufacture to styling to forecasting.

Her namesake shop is an expression of her insider status and expertise. Kohan is so spot-on about what her affluent fans will buy that since opening in 2005, she's never had to put anything on sale; it all sells out. It also helps that Kohan embraces a timeless aesthetic. Nothing on the racks looks like it's referencing any specific fad or era.

Another advantage is that the majority of the pieces are exclusives. Kohan likes to showcase new talent and essentially becomes such a champion of the designers she discovers that once they hit it big, they continue to either offer her first dibs on new items or create pieces especially for her shop. Kohan's was the first store to carry Mexican jewelry maker Gabriela Artigas, and although Artigas has since opened her own L.A. boutique, she still collaborates with Kohan on designs. The shop also carries exclusives by the imaginative Dutch duo Viktor & Rolf, Canadian Sid Neigum, and Juan Carlos Obando, a Colombian-born, Los Angeles-based former art director who has quickly found success. He and Kohan often team up to create custom pieces.

Not surprisingly, almost everything in Des Kohan, including the Neilah Meyers artwork featuring stags and hummingbirds that adorn the walls, is pricey. But these are investment pieces; the kind of stuff that never gets donated to Goodwill.

Address 671 Cloverdale Avenue Los Angeles, CA 90036, +1 323.857.0200,
www.deskohan.com, order@deskohan.com | **Getting there** I-10 to Fairfax Avenue.
Metered street parking. | **Hours** Mon–Sat 11am–6pm, Thurs 11am–7pm

26__Deus Ex Machina

Gods of motorcycle culture

The custom motorcycle is a California staple and many of the best-known builders either start out in the state or come west for inspiration. The Australian lifestyle company Deus Ex Machina (Latin / Greek calque meaning "god from the machine"), which has its only American retail outpost in Los Angeles, is known for its mind-blowing bikes. They are coveted by enthusiasts; and celebrities like Orlando Bloom, Ryan Reynolds, and Bruce Springsteen line up to pay $60,000 a pop to own one, which, according to the *Los Angeles Times*, is underpriced when you consider the hundreds of hours that go into production. The *Times* also said Deus and its U.S. master builder Michael "Woolie" Woolaway have earned "the reputation for building the nation's finest custom-made motorcycles."

The Deus store is all about celebrating that reputation. Located in Venice and billing itself as an "emporium of postmodern activities," it's a coffee shop, a hangout joint, a clothing store, and a surf shop, all rolled into one. The cafe drives traffic on most days, brewing Handsome Roasters, a local cult favorite. On the weekends the grill might be in full effect, with burgers or kebabs on the menu. And once a month the parking lot hosts "Sunday mass" with live music and food, attended by "sinners, winners, and hodads" with bikes, vintage cars, and kids in tow.

The Deus-branded apparel is pricey, but it's the lifestyle you're really buying. There are sweaters, board shorts, motocross shirts, goggles, and more. The Deus trucker hat has become a signature L.A. accessory.

This isn't the only motorcycle party in town of course. But what sets Deus Ex Machina apart is the meticulously coordinated effort that goes into everything: amazing coffee, apparel and accessories from top-notch designers, and gourmet food, all styled to perfection. And all in the name of worshipping the best custom bikes money can buy.

27 Diddy Riese

Tastes like home

There isn't a more enduring symbol of happy childhood memories than freshly baked cookies straight out of the oven. They represent Mom and innocence and basically all that is good in the world. Los Angeles college students, often living far from home, can quench their youthful cravings at Diddy Riese, a shop that sells cookies made from scratch all day, every day, for just 35 cents each.

After more than 30 years in the business, Diddy Riese is a local institution and its conscientious owner, Mark Perry, is a hometown hero. Perry's cookies, which come in ten Mom-approved varieties – white chocolate / macadamia nut is the fanciest combination available – are big, moist, and delicious. You can get three for a dollar, a half dozen for two dollars, or a "Diddy Dozen" for four. Add your choice of ice cream between two cookies for a custom-designed ice-cream sandwich for just $1.75. Diddy Riese also sells homemade brownies (with or without nuts) for 75 cents each, and big, fluffy Hawaiian shaved ice for $1 (pile on a scoop of ice cream for 50 cents more).

The student-friendly prices are the reason for the long lines, although the service has been honed to a science and everything moves along at a steady clip. But it's the familiar flavors of childhood that keep everyone coming back again and again.

Perry is at the store every day overseeing the large orders that have become de rigueur for local university and company parties. He has fielded offers from potential business partners offering franchise riches, and while he won't rule it out entirely (it might make a good retirement plan one day after all), he says it would be impossible to maintain his made-from-scratch standards if he was overseeing multiple locations.

So for now, college kids from campuses all around the county still have to make the trek here to Westwood whenever they have a hankering for a taste of home.

Address 926 Broxton Avenue, Los Angeles, CA 90024, +1 310.208.0448, www.diddyriese.com | Getting there I-405 to Wilshire Boulevard. Metered street parking. | **Hours** Mon–Thurs 11am–12am, Fri 11am–1am, Sat 12pm–1am, Sun 12pm–12am

28_ Elyse Walker

Get a red-carpet look

Designers may make the clothes but stylists make the look. The hand of a great stylist can take an outfit from merely expensive to "best dressed" chic. At Elyse Walker, anyone can get the star stylist treatment. This is a destination shop that's focused on the makeover experience. The store's eponymous owner is known for her styling prowess, catering to jet-setting clients and a celebrity following that includes Jennifer Garner, Kate Hudson, and supermodel Amber Valletta.

The staff is trained in the art of putting together the perfect look, and potential clients can make an appointment with one of these in-house gurus after checking out their profiles on the store's website, which offers information such as descriptions of their signature looks ("Parisienne chic meets rock and roll," or "a mix of prep and edge"), and favorite movies, vacation spots, and hangout activities – the kinds of details that might inspire a sympatico connection.

Occupying almost a full block of storefronts, Elyse Walker is essentially three connected boutiques, one focused on shoes and accessories, the others on couture and contemporary. You'll find pieces from top-of-the-heap houses like Alexander McQueen and Lanvin, as well as up-and-coming designers who are enjoying buzz for an innovative fashion "do." This makes the store a good place to figure out how to mix and match edgier statement pieces and more casual wear to create something truly individual.

The shop's Pacific Palisades neighborhood is like the conservative cousin of the three other millionaire communities it connects – Santa Monica, Brentwood, and Malibu. Nestled above the Pacific Ocean in the foothills of the Santa Monica mountains, the area gives off both a beachy vibe and a bit of wilderness cool. Equestrians love the neighborhood, and they can ride into Will Rogers State Park, where the home of the cowboy actor still stands, open to the public.

Address 15306 Antioch Street, Pacific Palisades, CA 90272, +1 310.230.8882,
www.elysewalker.com, elyse@elysewalker.com | Getting there CA-SR1/Pacific Coast
Highway to Temescal Canyon Road. Metered street parking. | Hours Mon–Sat
10am–6pm, Sun 12pm–5pm

29__Erewhon

If they sell it, it's got to be good for you

Erewhon is a 19th-century novel by Samuel Butler about a fictional country of the same name (pronounced air-won, it's an anagram of *nowhere*), which is a dystopia disguised as a utopia. Machines are banned, lest their artificial intelligence surpass humans' natural smarts, and sickness is a crime – citizens are responsible for making sure their bodies are fit and able.

Erewhon is also a supermarket that embraces a gentler version of the same health philosophy. Instead of leaving people to fend for themselves, this emporium is devoted to making a wholesome diet as easy as possible. Ever picked up something "natural" in your local grocery store, only to read the label and realize it's anything but? That won't happen here. Typical additives, preservatives, and flavorings like yeast extract, sodium benzoate, MSG, and high-fructose corn syrup are banned from Erewhon's shelves. Instead they stock only local, fresh, and truly all-natural foods, with the promise that everything the store sells is good for you.

The great news is that Erewhon offers a healthy version of just about anything you'd find at your local supermarket, including, as is customary in Los Angeles, beer and wine. There's an outstanding bulk/raw section, a refrigerator full of ready-to-go vegan meals, a large selection of gluten-free products, and arguably the world's best tonic and juice bar.

Popular drinks include the Jing City tonic, with herbs like deer antler, eucommia, and cordyceps, and the Golden Latte, with turmeric, ginger, and cardamon. There are superfood "ice creams" and smoothies like the Green Goddess, featuring spirulina, chlorella, and almond butter. But don't worry if the properties of herbal tonics and probiotic shots escape you. The staff will happily walk you through some recommendations. Or you can always just play it safe and opt for a classic combo, like apples, carrots, and beets.

Address 7660 Beverly Boulevard, Los Angeles, CA 90036, Phone +1 323.937.0777,
www.erewhonmarket.com, customerservice@erewhonmarket.com | Getting there I-10
to La Brea Avenue. Parking garage. | Hours Daily 11am–7pm

30 _ Fisherman's Outlet

Where L.A. communes

If you lunch at Fisherman's Outlet anytime between noon and 2pm, there's likely to be a line out the door. Don't worry, it moves quickly. And that queue is part of the experience. Just look who's standing on it: all of Los Angeles. From construction workers to college students to Hollywood producers and everyone in between, it's one of those few places where L.A. sheds its status barriers and becomes a community, standing (then sitting) shoulder to shoulder.

What's everyone here for? Heaping plates of fresh seafood: deep fried, charbroiled, cooked into chowders, and chopped into salads. Salmon, halibut, swordfish, roughy, bass, tilapia – it's all on the menu and it's all good. Everyone swears by the panko-crusted giant shrimp, but you really can't go wrong with any order. There are combos to choose from and almost everything comes with either fries and coleslaw or rice and spicy sauce. Nothing costs more than $20. Did I mention that it's all good?

Fisherman's Outlet started as a fish market in 1961, then expanded to include a restaurant. The eatery is staffed by about a dozen men who keep the lunch line moving. They work so fast and with such confident enthusiasm that it's natural to think they might screw up your order, but that almost never happens.

Something that nearly everyone who frequents the restaurant will tell you is that it takes a while to remember its name. The surrounding industrial neighborhood is also so nondescript that it takes a few trips to pinpoint exactly which block it's on. Lucky then, that all you have to say is, "The fish place – downtown L.A.," and anyone who's been there will give you directions (you can even Google that and Fisherman's Outlet will pop up!).

So get on that line. They close at 3:30pm, so it's not as if you can come back at a less-busy time anyway. Plus, this is a great place to meet some folks you may not otherwise.

Address 529 S Central Avenue, Los Angeles, CA 90013, +1 213.627.7231,
www.fishermansoutlet.net | Getting there I-10 to Central Avenue. Private parking lot. |
Hours Mon–Sat 10am–3:30pm

31_Fitzsu

Before you say "I do"

A wedding lasts one day. The items on a wedding registry, however, will stick around year after year after year. Design experts David "Fitz" FitzGerald and Su Sazama, recognizing that the process of creating a gift list had become a source of debilitating stress for couples planning the ultimate merger, came to the rescue with a better way to register, and in a better place – their home.

Fitzsu exists in the married couple's beautiful mid-city Los Angeles house, where items for sale are in use, on display, or in stock in their backyard warehouse. Couples who make an appointment need not fret about choosing the right place settings or needing specialized serving platters. Instead they can spend as much as time as they want being skillfully guided through offerings of everything needed to turn a house into a home.

The couple settled on the idea for their business when they themselves were preparing to tie the knot and couldn't find a registry that catered to their taste for contemporary, modern design accessories. They ended up begging several independent stores to let them register for specific items. After opening and closing stores in Los Angeles and Palm Springs, they settled on the home-front concept. Couples get frazzled in store environments because they feel pressured to make a decision while they have the salesperson's attention. At Fitzsu the low-key surroundings and focused advice make for a thoroughly pleasant experience.

Fitzsu stocks brands like Rosenthal, Alessi, Sambonet, and When Objects Work, among many others. And if a client yearns for something unusual, chances are they'll know where to find it. Of course you don't have to be planning a trip down the aisle to use their service – you don't even have to come to the "store." They will happily ship samples of dinnerware, chosen from their website, for clients to try out at home. But why pass up an opportunity to play house?

32 Freehand

Giving artisans the upper hand

Carol Sauvion, the owner of Freehand, is a goddess among craft makers. A former potter, she has been selling and representing American artisans at her gallery store for more than 30 years and is a sought-after speaker and consultant. She is also the award-winning creator of *Craft in America*, a long-running, award-winning series on public television that seeks out extraordinary artists and gives context to their techniques and traditions.

The store offers a comprehensive sampling of the kinds of handiwork that Sauvion champions. She opened her doors on West Third Street in 1980, before the neighborhood had experienced its transformation into a local shopping mecca. Ignoring naysayers who didn't think enough customers would be interested in handmade projects, Sauvion instead reintroduced Angelenos to contemporary artisans who, in the traditions of Tiffany glass and Rookwood pottery, are continuously working to further elevate materials, production, and American Craft as a sector.

The items for sale here aren't what usually come to mind when the term "arts and crafts" is bandied about. Everything is so exquisitely designed and created that it's hard to believe, even on close inspection, that these are handmade goods.

A sampling of the California artists represented at the store includes Michael Bayes, who was born in London but now lives in the California desert and makes delicate gold earrings embellished with natural stones; Claudia Grau, known as a pioneer of fabric recycling, whose reconstructed, hand-dyed pieces are one of a kind; and ceramist David Gurney, whose brightly painted terra-cotta celebrates nature. There are, of course, also scores of artists from other parts of the country, like New Englander Randall Darwall, who makes handwoven silk scarves in rich, earthy colors. The exquisite objects you'll find at Freehand are proof positive that American craft is alive and thriving.

Address 8413 W Third St, Los Angeles, CA 90048, +1 323.655.2607, www.freehand.com |
Getting there I-10 to La Cienega. Parking behind store. Metered street parking. | Hours
Mon–Sat 11am–6pm

33 Galco's Old World Grocery

Because carbonation makes everything better

Galco's has been around in some form since 1897, founded by partners Galiotto and Cortopassi as an Italian imports business. Louis Nese ran it as Galco's Old World Grocery, selling staples for the Italian kitchen and deli sandwiches, before handing the reins to his son, John.

About 15 years ago, John was struggling to keep the store afloat. Big chains dominated food distribution channels and he couldn't compete with the discount prices they were offering. A lifelong soda fan (he saw a naturally carbonated spring on a family vacation when he was a child and still talks about it), Nese had grown up hearing his father's stories about his days as a soda jerk. He couldn't imagine his store without pop, but an argument with his Pepsi salesman about pricing led him in an unexpected direction. The salesman's rebuke that customers would revolt if he didn't carry their "demand item" gave Nese the idea to partner with small soda manufacturers to turn Galco's into a destination for fans of hard-to-find brands.

Beginning with 25 different varieties, he now carries 750 sodas from around the world. The store is part nostalgia, part hipster niche. There's Manhattan Special Pure Espresso Coffee Soda, which has been made by the same New York family since 1895, and Red Ribbon Cherry Supreme, the "cherriest" soda since 1904. A new-wave brand is Sweet Blossom floral sodas, available in Rose, Jasmine, Lavender, and Elderflower. The same company also produces the award-winning Mr. Q. Cumber (guess what flavor).

Another genius addition to Galco's is the DIY soda creation station. For $2.99 a bottle the Soda Pop Stop lets customers dispense carbonated water, add any one of dozens of flavored syrups, and cap it for a custom beverage. Nese has also added specialty beers (750 kinds) and a selection of dessert wines, including plum and chocolate.

Address 5702 York Boulevard, Los Angeles, CA 90042, +1 323.255.7115,
www.galcos.com | Getting there SR 110N to Avenue 52, Highland Park. Parking lot. |
Hours Mon–Sat 9am–6:30pm, Sun 9am–4pm

34_ GameHäus
For serious (board) gamers

Nine people showed up to Robert Cron and Terry Chiu's first board game night. But pretty soon they were scrambling to find spaces that could accommodate the 50 to 60 people who regularly came to play. Cron, a costume designer, and Chiu, a graphic artist who designed menu templates for DVDs, began to dream up their ideal gaming paradise, a place where they could happily geek out for 12 hours a day playing board games.

For the faithful, Cron and Chiu have stocked GameHäus with 900 games (and counting) from around the world. There are Eurogames, which eschew the American emphasis on luck. These are usually made from simple materials, depend more on strategy than a roll of the dice, and allow all players to survive to the end. There are also Ameritrash games, with brilliant designs, stories of heroes, and toy tie-ins. Plenty of retro classics like Monopoly and Risk fill the shelves, as do a plethora of 21st-century newbies like Twilight Struggle, a two-player warfare card game that can go on for hours. GameHäus hosts a Wednesday Night Board Game 101 class to explain the rules of complex games like Cyclades, where players race to build cities in ancient Greece.

GameHäus is also a coffee shop, which Cron says is primarily aimed at giving the uninitiated a reason to come in and get inculcated. They sell sandwiches, pizza, and bakery items, as well, because even intense gamers need to come up for snacks. While the clientele is mostly groups of young people who could otherwise be whiling away their time at a bar or a club, this is also a great place for a family game night, especially if you're trying to disengage your tweens or teens from their ubiquitous screens.

The price to play is five dollars per person, whether you plan to stay for five minutes or five hours. There's also, deliberately, no Wi-Fi. No distractions allowed; you have to be in it to win it.

Address 1800 S Brand Boulevard, Glendale, CA 91204, +1 818.937.9061, www.gamehauscafe.com | **Getting there** I-5 to Glendale Boulevard. Street parking. Valet parking sometimes available (see website). | **Hours** Tues–Thurs 11am–11pm, Fri–Sat 11am–12am, Sun 11am–9pm

35___Giant Robot

Beyond Hello Kitty

Nowadays, it seems impossible to walk more than a few blocks in Los Angeles without passing yet another store dedicated to Japanese pop culture. It wasn't always that way. When Eric Nakamura was growing up in West L.A., he couldn't find any place that reliably carried the art he loved, an aesthetic that marries punk, minimalism, and cuteness. So after graduating from UCLA with a degree in East Asian Studies, Nakamura started *Giant Robot* magazine, which introduced hip Japanese art, artists, and celebrities to America and helped launch a revolution.

In 2001, Nakamura opened the Giant Robot Store on Sawtelle Boulevard, known as Little Osaka because its concentration of Japanese businesses is second only to downtown's Little Tokyo. Giant Robot was among the first U.S. stores to feature artists like Takashi Murakami and Yoshi Nara. Giant Robot also sparked the Uglydoll craze when David Horvath, the designer, brought a prototype to the store and Nakamura immediately placed an order. The dolls are now popular around the world and for the last two years, Giant Robot has hosted a fan convention called UglyCon.

The store also sells graphic T-shirts, hoodies, and hats; geek culture toys and figurines; robots and robot art; and an assortment of items that possess the anime aesthetic (ninja bandages anyone?). For several years Nakamura worked on scaling up the business, opening stores in San Francisco and New York, only to scale back down to just the Sawtelle location. Still, Giant Robot's influence is far from diminished. Maybe because the proliferation of Japanese cute has started to reach saturation, Nakamura's carefully curated offerings stand out as a best-of collection.

Nakamura also orchestrates shows of Japanese pop art at his own GR2 Gallery, and for museums like the Oakland Museum of California and the Japanese American National Museum.

Jeni Yang
$400

Address 2015 Sawtelle Boulevard, Los Angeles, CA 90025, +1 310.478.1819, www.giantrobot.com | Getting there I-405 to Santa Monica Boulevard. Metered street parking. | Hours Mon–Sat 11:30am–8pm, Sun 12pm–7pm

Jason Limon
350

36_ Gogosha

A spectacular selection of shades

If you're going to look the part in L.A., you'll need a pair of signature sunnies, and when it comes to knowing what's hot, Julia Gogosha is visionary. A former optician, Gogosha also worked as a rep for eyewear brands and gained a reputation as a foremost authority on the coolest trends and styles. In 2008 she opened Gogosha Optique, a sleek, bright-white storefront that pays homage to the world's most interesting eyeglasses.

In a city that averages 329 days of sun per year, sunglasses aren't just for the arbiters of cool, and many Angelenos take their eyewear very seriously. Gogosha's goal is to give customers the kind of experience and selection they could never find at a Sunglass Hut or LensCrafters, so she only carries lines that are made using sophisticated production methods, that stand out as statement pieces, or are from freshly crowned designers of the moment – like Ahlem Manai-Platt, the L.A.-based Parisian of Tunisian heritage who names her styles after places in the French capital – Belleville, St. Germain, Palais Royal; or fashionista favorites Thierry Lasry and Gareth Leight.

Gogosha also stocks old-school lines like Cutler and Gross and Oliver Goldsmith, brands that helped elevate sunglasses from merely eye protection to essential fashion accessories. But it's not just about the shades. Gogosha is also serious about prescription spectacles, and will expertly insert lenses into frames from designers like Shiloh Rapp, whose handmade glasses can only be found in about 30 stores worldwide; Xavier Derome, who carves each of his lunettes out of a single solid block of acetate; and Claire Goldsmith, the great-granddaughter of the Oliver Goldsmith founder who is making her own mark.

With prices running between $225 and $1000, the goal is to make sure that – from materials to craftsmanship to finish – the glasses fit perfectly and reflect the wearer's personality.

Address 3208½ W Sunset Boulevard, Los Angeles, CA 90026, +1 323-660-1122, www.gogosha.com | Getting there US-101 to Rampart. Metered street parking. | Hours Sun–Mon 12pm–5pm, Tues–Sat 11am–7pm

37_Gold Bug

The art of nature

This shop was cleverly named for an Edgar Allan Poe story about a golden bug and a hunt for treasure, and as soon as you step inside, you'll understand why.

Gold Bug is precisely curated to offer high-end art that is either made from nature or inspired by it. The eccentric and intriguing offerings range from Evan Chambers's steampunk lamps, made to look like bug-eyed aliens that stand on ostrich or hawk feet or octopus tentacles; to Anthony Lent's golden tree frog earrings, moonface rings, and scarab pendant diamond necklaces; to Christopher Marley's meticulously restored, brightly colored insects, birds, and serpents – all that have died of natural causes. Some items – a stuffed, crown-wearing beaver or an exquisite necklace made from 40,000-year-old woolly mammoth teeth – are morbidly fascinating and beautiful. Yet others, like the neo-Victorian découpage home accessories or objects delicately carved from shiny pencil graphite (yes, you can write with them!), are wonderfully imaginative.

Gold Bug is owned by Stacey Coleman, Shelley Kimball, and their daughter Theodora Coleman, who first came to Los Angeles to attend Occidental College. Their trips to visit Theodora became so frequent, that Stacy and Shelley eventually sold their business and moved in with their daughter. Gold Bug, which they opened in 2007, evokes the life they left behind on picturesque Orcas, one of the rustic San Juan Islands nestled off the coast of Washington. Known as the emerald isle, it is a hilly, forested paradise for lovers of the outdoors, like the Colemans and the dozens of artists they partner with.

Gold Bug is located in the heart of "Old Town" Pasadena. Outside its doors, the streets bustle with traffic and tourists, but inside the shop, you're transported to a magical cabinet of curiosities – a modern celebration of the forests, the oceans, the skies, and the creatures that beautify them.

Address 22 E Union Street, Pasadena, CA 91103, +1 626.744.9963,
www.goldbugpasadena.com, info@goldbugpasadena.com | Getting there SR 110N to
Fair Oaks. SR 134 to Del Mar Boulevard. Parking garage. | Hours Mon–Sat 11am–6pm,
Sun 12pm–5pm

38__ Gornik & Drucker

A modern barbershop with an old-school pedigree

On a visit to his home state of California while still in office, Ronald Reagan stopped in to the barbershop he used to frequent, first as a young actor, then as the state's governor. The president insisted on paying the $35 for his haircut, until he realized he didn't have any money on him. Neither did any of his secret service detail. So Reagan had a check sent over posthaste from his personal account. Owner William Gornik displays the uncashed check and its envelope on the shop's wall along with other memorabilia from the life of one of the business's most loyal clients.

Reagan's longtime barber was actually the late Harry Drucker, who established this Beverly Hills barbering business in 1936 and also regularly groomed Clark Gable, Tyrone Power, Frank Sinatra, and Bugsy Siegel. In 1998, Drucker recruited Gornik, a younger star barber who had been his main rival.

When the luxury Montage Hotel opened in Beverly Hills' golden triangle neighborhood in 2008, the developers offered Gornik space in its lower lobby as a way to draw in his well-heeled clients. It harkens back to the days when haberdashers put barbershops in the backs of their stores to attract men who weren't regular shoppers. The arrangement has been beneficial, and Gornik has since closed the original shop.

The service here is old school meets new school. You'll get a haircut, razor shave, and, if you'd like, a facial that's billed as "better than two hours' sleep." There are only two chairs so it's best to make an appointment. The décor conveys the business's historical significance with dark woods, leather upholstery, and vintage fixtures. Gornik offers its own grooming products, including shaving cream and bay rum aftershave. And for $100 to $300 you can take home an Italian leather dopp kit filled with the store's product line. That's in addition to the $130 it'll run you for a shave and a haircut these days.

Address 225 North Canon Drive, Beverly Hills, CA 90210, +1 310.860.7819, www.gornikanddrucker.com, barbers@gornikanddrucker.com | **Getting there** I-10 to Robertson. I-405 to Santa Monica Boulevard. Free valet parking. | **Hours** Mon–Sat 8am–7pm, Sun 12pm–5pm

39_ Grand Central Market
Center of the downtown revival

Grand Central Market has been around since 1917, making it one of the country's oldest – and largest – public markets. Located on the ground floor of the historic Homer Laughlin building, it has always been a reflection of the city zeitgeist. These days that means that after decades of decay and slump, it's part of a downtown revival. In the surrounding streets, flophouse hotels have been converted to swanky lofts, gallery row is encroaching on skid row, and celebrity chefs lure suburbanites to the city core. Yet there's still a lingering grittiness that refuses to recede without a fight.

Grand Central Market reflects all this. There's a designer flower studio, My Secret Garden, known for elaborately artistic arrangements; gourmet coffee and carbonated ice tea at G&B Coffee; innovative fast-casual concepts like Eggslut, Berlin Currywurst, and Madcapra – a chef-driven take on falafel. You can also enjoy a wine pairing with mussels, scallops, clams, sea urchin, and, yes, oysters, at the Oyster Gourmet, which is led by Christophe Happillon, who is billed as the city's only master *écailler* (shellfish & oyster specialist).

Despite the makeover, Grand Central Market, like downtown, is still clinging to its past. Not too long ago, it was largely patronized by locals (mostly Latino), who came here for fresh fruit, spices, and authentic homestyle foods like pupusas and tacos. Although it's become the domain of foodies these days, some old-school vendors help it retain its original spirit. Grand Central Jewelry, for instance, owned by the Serrano family, opened in 1983 and continues to hold on to its small piece of increasingly valuable real estate. The store sells shiny, mass-manufactured gold and gemstone jewelry and also offers watch repair and key copying. The Serranos also run Sarita's Pupuseria, which makes a dozen varieties of the Salvadoran stuffed griddled corn cakes and helps bring in longtime downtown denizens.

Address 317 S Broadway, Los Angeles, CA 90013, +1 213.620.1864,
www.grandcentralmarket.com | Getting there I-110 to Fourth Street. Parking garage. |
Hours Sun–Wed 8am–6pm, Thurs–Sat 9am–9pm

40__Grist & Toll

Local flour power

Back in the days before global, industrialized food production and distribution, the flour mill was an important, central meeting place where farmers brought their grist (grain) for grinding, and the miller kept some of it as toll (payment). The establishment of a mill was an indication of an area's growth potential. The Capitol Milling Company, for example, was built in the early 1800s, when the city was still a Spanish outpost with a population of less than 1000, and was L.A.'s oldest operating business when it finally closed at the turn of this century.

Grist & Toll was established in that spirit of community, in this case engaging the growing number of home bakers who are interested in using flour made from artisan whole wheat and grains. This "urban mill" is right down the road from a Whole Foods, and 10 minutes away from El Molino Viejo (the Old Mill), the oldest commercial building in all of Southern California. The owners like to say that Grist & Toll is the newest old idea in the world.

The seed for Grist & Toll grew out of pastry chef Nan Kohler's own obsession with her main ingredient. Discovering how difficult it was to find a variety of locally produced flour, she and her business partner invested in a wooden mill from Austria that looks like a work of art. It sits in a pristine space and shoots out flour made from Red Fife, Sonora, Spelt, and other grains from Kohler's farmer partners.

Grist & Toll's mill room is separated from its retail shop by a large picture window. Kohler knew her customers would be curious about the milling facility and she's happy to indulge them. She hosts workshops and lectures and writes a deeply informative, recipe-filled blog to encourage both grain production by farmers and the use of local flour by home bakers. Kohler says education is at the heart of what she does. Call it the new development mission of the local flour mill.

Address 990 S Arroyo Parkway, Suite 1, Pasadena, CA 91105, +1 626.441.7400, www.gristandtoll.com, info@gristandtoll.com | **Getting there** CA-110N becomes South Arroyo Parkway. Parking lot. | **Hours** Wed–Sat 11am–5pm

41 Grow Native Nursery
The three Ps: plants, parrots, and "play ball!"

There's a frequent misconception that native California plants are coarse, drought resistant, and non-flowering. Not so. The state has a variety of climates, from the moist habitats of its Redwood forests to the arid expanses of Death Valley, and its plants are just as diverse.

Grow Native Nursery, located in the gardens of the Veterans Administration Complex, is a nonprofit that cultivates and sells California-bred plants and seeds. It's an outpost of the Rancho Santa Ana Botanic Garden of Claremont, a college town located 50 miles east of downtown L.A. The botanic garden, which was established in 1927, is dedicated to studying, growing, and conserving native California plant species, especially the 40 percent that are endemic to the state and the more than 1100 plants that are considered endangered. Its Los Angeles location, established in 2010, revived the abandoned gardens at the back of the sprawling Veterans complex, cultivating 10,000 square feet of growing space and employing vets to harvest and pot the plants.

The grounds are a great place to while away an afternoon. The garden abuts Jackie Robinson Stadium, home to the UCLA Bruins baseball team, and it's possible to sit on the nursery's outdoor benches and take in a home game. At one end of the garden is Serenity Park, a sanctuary for rescued parrots that serves as a therapy center for the veterans who maintain it. Whenever there are vets present, the gates are opened and the public is welcomed in to engage the gregarious feathered friends and the men and women who benefit from their company.

Besides selling plants, the nursery offers free workshops every month on topics like "The Most Colorful CA Native Plants" and "Replacing Your Lawn." Lawns, it turns out, aren't native to California. They were modeled on the royal gardens of Europe and watering them accounts for 50 percent of L.A.'s water use. Now that's just not natural.

Address 100 Davis Avenue, Los Angeles, CA 90049, +1 424.234.0481, www.rsabg.org/gnn-westwood, gnnwestla@rsabg.org | Getting there I-405 to Wilshire Boulevard. Parking lot. | Hours Wed–Sun 10am–4:30pm

42___Guild

Where black is always the new black

When Michael Rosen was starting out in the clothing business in the '70s – working as a manufacturing agent – he suggested to his bosses that they consider going to Asia. They suggested that he didn't know what he was talking about. Six months later, he received an apology and a plane ticket to China.

Rosen must have passed off that prescience gene to his son Christopher, his partner in Guild, one of the most sleekly curated clothing stores in L.A. Christopher conceived Guild in 2010, when Venice's main drag, Abbot Kinney Boulevard (named for the man who tried to replicate the Italian archipelago in Southern California), was still a bastion of bohemian handcrafted goods. He sensed the neighborhood had more sophisticated tastes than it was getting credit for, and time has proven him right.

Guild carries established, international superstar designers such as Ann Demeulemeester, Rick Owens, and Mihara Yasuhiro, as well as hip new lines from the likes of artist turned actor turned designer Greg Lauren, who doesn't share his famous uncle Ralph's love of prep. They also carry hot denim brands like R13 and AMO. Father and son share the duties of the store with their wives Susan and Christine. Michael likes to say that between the four of them they've got more than 100 years' experience in fashion manufacturing, sourcing, and merchandising.

The Rosens' aesthetic is definitely rock 'n' roll, so black is always the new black at Guild. The boutique brings a bit of New York edge to Abbot Kinney's eclectic mix of shops, restaurants, and galleries. The boulevard is less than a mile long but with more than 100 independent retailers, it can take hours to make your way from one end of the street to the other. The relatively short expanse makes this a great walking area. If you find a parking spot, nab it – parking can be next to impossible, so some stores have even started providing complimentary valet.

Address 1335 Abbot Kinney Boulevard, Venice, CA 90291, +1 310.396.8300, www.guildla.com | Getting there I-405 to Venice Boulevard. Metered street parking. | Hours Mon–Fri 11am–7pm, Sat 11am–6pm, Sun 12pm–6pm

43 H. Lorenzo

The home of cutting edge

If you've ever flipped through the pages of *Vogue* and coveted the featured cutting-edge styles, then H. Lorenzo will leave you breathless. The store's racks are meticulously hung with luxurious creations by Comme des Garçons, Boris Bidjan Saberi, Haider Ackerman, and other designers of the moment. The shop gives off a distinctly goth vibe and is popular with the trend setters of L.A.'s underground fashion scene. They breeze through here for inspiration and to snag an authentic high-end piece, the kind that can elevate street wear to an art form.

H. Lorenzo is a family affair, owned by Lorenzo and Sharona Hadar and run by their son Mac. The older Hadars met while serving in the Israeli army and moved to the United States with the dream of opening a fashion business. Lorenzo worked as a handyman to earn the money they would eventually invest, first in a shoe store and then in their eponymous boutique. The store has been on Sunset Boulevard for more than 30 years.

The business is made up of two spaces – one showcasing women's clothing and the other men's – which are bisected by two restaurants: Le Petit Four, which fans of HBO's *Entourage* will recognize as one of Vince and his posse's favorite haunts, and Sushiya. Mac Hadar is the menswear buyer and the store is a reflection of his personal style. He favors designers like Christophe Lemaire and Yohji Yamamoto and seeks out brands that might not yet have a following in the States. For instance, H. Lorenzo was the first retailer outside of Japan to carry Julius, the avant-garde, mostly black line of Tatsuro Horikawa.

Collectively the pieces at H. Lorenzo seem to line up like the greatest hits of Paris Fashion Week. Just a few choice pieces can upgrade your entire wardrobe to rock-star chic. For those without deep pockets, the end-of-the-year clearance sale is a godsend, with discounts of 50 to 70 percent off.

Address 8660 W Sunset Boulevard, West Hollywood, CA 90069, +310.659.0058, www.hlorenzo.com | Getting there I-10 to La Cienega. Parking lot. | Hours Daily 10am–7pm

44_ H. Savinar Luggage

Equipment for road warriors

All frequent travelers know that quality luggage is not a luxury, it's a necessity. These globe-trotters are always the early adopters of the technologies that make bags lighter or easier to tote through today's massive airports and train stations. In the early '70s it was Bernard Sadow's invention of rolling suitcases. The U.S. Luggage executive applied four wheels and a strap to what were then traditional hard-sided, latched bags. Next it was Rollaboards, invented by pilot Robert Plath, who would form the company Travelpro. Plath introduced the two-wheeled upright case with the telescoping handle that became ubiquitous, as did its soft sided zippered designs. These days it's all about durable, high-tech materials – flexible polycarbonates and lightweight carbon fibers.

In Los Angeles, road warriors know the only place to shop for top-of-the-line travel gear at a great price is H. Savinar, an unassuming brick-faced store that has always been at the forefront of luggage innovations. You'll find the latest upgrades from companies like Rimowa, Hartmann, Swiss Army, Eagle Creek, and Briggs & Riley, plus all the department-store brands, including Samsonite, Delsey, and Travelpro. Prices range from $40 to more than $1000. But the real difference is the level of service. The store's motto is that everybody leaves happy, so they pay incredible attention to customers seeking something they don't have on the floor. And they'll do everything possible to source it. They also offer personalization, adding monograms or logos to luggage, briefcases, duffels, and even leather-bound notebooks.

This is a family-owned business started in 1916 by Harry Savinar, who passed it on to his sons, Harold and Hyman, and their extended family. At one time, half of the staff were Savinars. Nonagenarian Harold still comes in to do a little work now and again and to say hello to his frequent-flyer customers.

Address 4625 W Washington Boulevard, Los Angeles, CA 90016, +1 323.938.2501,
www.savinarluggage.com, savinarluggage@sbcglobal.net | Getting there I-10 to La Brea
Avenue or Crenshaw Boulevard. Private parking lot. | Hours Mon–Fri 9am–5pm,
Sat 10am–5pm

45_ Heath Ceramics
The art of everyday

Yes, Heath Ceramics is selling everyday household items. We all need cups and jugs and serving plates. But it would be impossible to label the items here as purely utilitarian. While they are the epitome of simplicity, the domes of the bowls just seem a little more regal than anything you'd find at a national chain, even the high-end ones. The handles of the cups are a bit longer, leaner, and more graceful; the tones are earthier, yet vibrant. And while items like vases are always meant to be decorative, the shapes at Heath are particularly surprising and eye catching. An elegant candle tray makes you realize that a device for holding a row of four tea lights is precisely what you've always needed (even if you didn't know it).

The beautiful products at Heath come from a storied history. The company was founded by legendary ceramist Edith Heath in 1948, when her first solo pottery show led to offers to buy her dinnerware. She and her husband established a factory in Sausalito, California, where the company still makes many of its minimalist artisan products.

Edith's pieces can be found in museum collections including New York's MoMA and LACMA in Los Angeles. She had a strong point of view, creating objects whose beauty lay in their clean lines and simple silhouettes. Her original Coupe line of dishes is still a standout bestseller, as is the Rim line, designed in 1960 to allow easy stacking.

Current owners Catherine Bailey and Robin Petravic have followed in the footsteps of Heath's beloved founder. Their Chez Panisse line, for example, was designed for use at Alice Waters' legendary Berkeley restaurant, known for local, organic cooking. And a collaboration with sewing company Alabama Chanin appears to be the perfect marriage of clay and embroidered cotton. It's all a continuation of the timeless aesthetic that Edith Heath embraced.

Address 7525 Beverly Boulevard, Los Angeles, CA 90036, +1 323.965.0800, www.heathceramics.com | **Getting there** I-10 to La Brea Avenue. Private parking lot. | **Hours** Mon–Sat 10am–6pm, Thurs 10am–7pm, Sun 12pm–6pm

46_ Hidden Treasures
A trove of vintage gold

In spirit, Hidden Treasures is the most unpretentious vintage store you'll find in Los Angeles. It's filled to the brim with anything that's worth anything, even if it's just a few dimes. There are real and fake furs at a variety of price points, marbles and sea glass, kitschy lamps and figurines, designer bags, no-name shoes, a bin full of scarves, a bevy of hats, photos, rings, and arrowheads.

The display, however, is beyond bombastic. Tucked into a corner on a turn of Topanga Canyon Boulevard, the shop is a sight to behold – a hippie version of a haunted house that seems to have been commandeered by pirates, with ghoulish figures on guard and a sparklingly dressed but offbeat mannequin greeting you at the door.

An outdoor trunk holds all kinds of clothing, on clearance for $1.75. Inside, the rooms have interesting nooks and the same kooky, joyful personality as the exterior. A Statue of Liberty lamp and desiccated snakeskin share a shelf and suddenly seem like must-have, complementary home accessories.

The store is frequented by everyone from celebrities and their stylists (it's possible to find genuine pieces from designers like Pucci, Oscar de la Renta, and more), to families in search of adventure. Topanga itself is like visiting another place and time. Nestled in the Santa Monica Mountains, it is only accessible by the canyon road and is known for its bohemian vibe. Surrounded by nature, it feels cut off from the rest of Los Angeles.

Topanga has long been a favorite outpost of creative types and is also a popular destination for hikers who come to explore the 36 miles of trails in Topanga State Park, which offers amazing views of the Pacific, and, at 14,000 acres, is considered the world's largest wildland within the boundaries of a major city. Its hidden treasures can be found below the trees as well as among the knickknacks.

Address 154 S Topanga Canyon Boulevard, Topanga, CA 90290 +1 310.455.2998 |
Getting there Pacific Coast Highway or US-101 to Topanga Canyon Boulevard.
Parking out front or next door. | Hours Daily 10:30am–6pm

47 High Voltage Tattoo
The hottest ink in L.A.

When celebrity tattoo artist Kat Von D named her shop High Voltage, she surely didn't realize just how hot things would get (literally – the shop had to be redesigned after an electrical fire ripped through the building, causing extensive damage). Today, people come from all over the world to get inked by Kat and her staff.

Von D grew up an hour east of L.A. and began tattooing as a teenager, earning recognition for astonishingly realistic black-and-white portraits. She became famous when she joined the cast of *Miami Ink*, the hit TLC reality show that helped take tattoo culture mainstream. Von D, with her striking good looks, sexy leather attire, and incredible artistry, was such a standout she earned her own spin-off series, *LA Ink*. Since then, she has branched off into clothing, jewelry, a line of makeup for Sephora, and signature tattoo designs, all available at Kat Von D's Wonderland, a retail store next to the tattoo parlor. Von D has also become a tabloid fixture for high-profile romances with fellow ink-covered celebs Nikki Sixx, Jesse James, and Deadmau5.

Star status aside, Kat Von D's fans flock to her shop because of the talent. As a rock 'n' roll town, Los Angeles has long been a bastion of tattoo culture. Many world-famous artists are based here so you have to be something special to stand out, and Von D is certainly that. There are countless examples of her work online and it helps that she has a long list of celebrity clients, including Miley Cyrus, Lady Gaga, and reportedly Beyonce. It's possible to walk into High Voltage and get tattooed on the spot, but with a minimum price of $200 (which helps insure the artists don't spend their days inking a slew of tourists in search of a one-of-a-kind souvenir), it's probably best to plan ahead. It'll cost a lot more to get Von D to tattoo you herself, but if you're serious about your body art, she's worth every penny.

48_Hiromi Paper, Inc.

A paper trail from Japan to the United States

Hiromi Katayama was already very knowledgeable about papermaking when she moved to America. As a mixed-media artist in Japan, she had developed an interest in *washi* – the country's 1000-year-old handmade paper tradition – and had studied with a master of the art. Made from *kozo* bark, *gampi*, and *mitsumata* bush as well as other natural fibers, *washi* is both softer and stronger than machine-made paper.

What Katayama didn't realize was that there was a great need in the Unites States for someone with her precise expertise. From her own work, Katayama understood the importance of having the right materials. While teaching *washi* at the University of California, Santa Barbara, Katayama began connecting artist friends to the old Japanese masters who could supply them with the best quality papers. Before long she was consulting for major institutions such as the Getty Museum and the Los Angeles County Museum of Art (LACMA), facilitating their acquisition of fine papers to be used in restoring and conserving valuable artwork.

Katayama opened Hiromi Paper in 1988 and the store is now considered the premiere source for *washi* in the country. Hiromi also sells other handmade paper from around the world, including Bhutan, Nepal, and Yucatan, Mexico, where the paper known as *Huun* (the Mayan word for "paper" as well as the tree that produces the fibers) had all but disappeared until artisans revived the tradition in the '80s. The store also sells its own specialty *kozo* (a 79-inch square sheet goes for about $400) and artists frequently custom-order handmade papers for individual projects. There's also an assortment of gifts, from adorable animal-shaped paper balloons to notebooks and other stationery. The papers carried here aren't just for artists, however. If your job hunt requires a nicely printed resume, a 10-pack of Asuka paper will set you apart from the rest of the crowd for less than $5.

KATAZOME
Handmade in Japan on Kozo
Size: 25"x 18"
$17.00 per full sheet
$8.40 Half Sheet
4-RO

KATAZOME
Handmade in Japan on Kozo
Size: 25"x 18"
$17.00 per full sheet
$8.40 Half Sheet
WA-6206

KATAZOME
Handmade in Japan on Kozo
Size: 25"x 18"
$17.00 per full sheet
$8.40 Half Sheet
WA-6201

KATAZOME
Handmade in Japan on Kozo
Size: 25"x 18"
$17.00 per full sheet
$8.40 Half Sheet
WA-6221

KATAZOME
Handmade in Japan on Kozo
Size: 25"x 18"
$17.00 per full sheet
$8.40 Half Sheet
WA-6231

KATAZOME
Handmade in Japan on Kozo
Size: 25"x 18"
$17.00 per full sheet
$8.40 Half Sheet
34-I

KATAZOME
Handmade in Japan on Kozo
Size: 25"x 18"
$17.00 per full sheet
$8.40 Half Sheet
34-RO

KATAZOME
Handmade in Japan on Kozo
Size: 25"x 18"
$17.00 per full sheet
$8.40 Half Sheet
34-HA

Address 2525 Michigan Avenue, Unit G-9, Santa Monica, CA 90404, +1 310.998.0098,
www.hiromipaper.com, washi@hiromipaper.com | Getting there I-10 to Cloverfield
Boulevard. Parking lot. | Hours Mon–Fri 10am–5pm, Sat 10am–6pm

49__Hollywood Smoke

Is a cigar really just a cigar?

Unlike the typical private cigar clubs in L.A., Hollywood Smoke happily welcomes everyone who walks in the door. It has all the desired trappings of a luxury lounge – buttery leather armchairs, and a well-stocked humidor with products from around the world – but is still an everyman's or everywoman's kind of place.

Owner Greg Shabazian was a cigar fan interested in getting into the business when, in 1996, he had the opportunity to open a cigar salon in a building owned by the future governor of California, Arnold Schwarzenegger. The Terminator had a restaurant on the top floor, and, as a well-known cigar aficionado, was thrilled to have access to a stash of stogies downstairs. The two businesses held cigar dinners for as many as 300 guests at a time.

Schwarzenegger has since moved on, but Shabazian continues to spread the gospel of cigars. He especially loves it when a newbie discovers his shop and he gets the chance to walk them through the proper smoking ritual: First, there's the cut – Shabazian cautions against snipping too much. Then there's the light, turning and roasting the end as you would a marshmallow over a campfire. Finally, there's the puff. Shabazian starts novices on a mild cigar so the flavor will be smooth and pleasant. The experienced smoker receives a different treatment. For her, Shabazian asks about her favorite brands, and then makes recommendations based on her preferred flavor profile.

Shabazian also hosts an online series called *The World of Cigars*, in which he visits growers and explains the art of cigar-making and its history. You'll learn all sorts of interesting trivia, such as the fact that a premium hand-rolled cigar will be touched at least 285 times by a human being during the manufacturing process.

There is no bar at Hollywood Smoke, but Shabazian will happily pour his guests a drink, something that perfectly complements the puff they select.

Address 3110 Main Street, Suite 106, Santa Monica, CA 90405 +1 310.396.1661 | **Getting there** I-10W to Fourth Street. Metered street parking. | **Hours** Mon–Wed 11am–10pm, Thurs 11am–11pm, Fri–Sat 11am–12am, Sun 12pm–10pm

50__Holy Grail
Sneaker heaven

If the terms Yeezy 2, Jordan Elevens, and Penny Foamposites don't sound like gibberish to you, the Holy Grail is where you should worship. This store specializes in brand-new, rare, and limited-edition kicks, the kinds that inspire the sneaker-obsessed to camp out overnight at Foot Locker locations in order to be first in line to snap up a new style.

For the uninitiated, here's an example of how collectible sports footwear can be: the Nike Air Yeezy 2 was a collaboration between the sportswear giant and rapper Kanye West, who also goes by the moniker "Yeezy." Nike issued 5,000 pairs of each of a handful of colors. One variety, called the Red Octobers, was released online only – without any warning – in February 2014, and sold out in minutes. Originally priced at $245, a pair of coveted Yeezy 2s was recently on sale at the Holy Grail for $4200. And they weren't even Red Octobers.

If there's a sneaker you can't live without, chances are you'll find it in pristine condition on the shelves of the Holy Grail. They also sell the latest lines endorsed by stars like Kobe Bryant, Kevin Durant, and Lebron James. But don't expect to shell out less than $250 if you want to walk out of the shop with happy feet. And if you're looking to sell rather than buy, you can also consign your kicks to the Holy Grail for a 20 percent commission.

The Holy Grail is located around the corner from the Staples Center, the arena where three of the Los Angeles home teams – the NBA Lakers, the Clippers, and the NHL Kings – play. The proximity is usually a boon for the shop. (Visitors moved by Magic Johnson's statue in the Staples courtyard might just be inspired to get some gear.) Except in 2009, that is, when the Lakers won the national championship and celebrating fans broke through the shop windows and set fire to all the shoes. Just imagine how the prices must have rocketed after that.

Address 604 W Pico Boulevard, Los Angeles, CA 90015, +1 213.746.6405,
www.holygrailgoods.com, info@holygrailgoods.com | Getting there I-110N to
Ninth Street. Street parking. | Hours Daily 11am–7pm

51___Homegirl Café

Eat well and save lives

Homegirl Café offers a farm-to-table menu, with Mexican influences. Chiliquiles are on the breakfast menu, and there's guacamole and tacos for lunch. Much of the greens are sourced from an urban farm out back, and a full bakery offers fresh bread, pastries, granola, and fruity preserves. It's all served in a beautiful, bright, and airy dining room. The service is gracious, and if you're in the downtown corridor near Union Station and Chinatown, it's a solidly good place to catch a bite.

But even all that is not what's truly special about this eatery. The first clue that there's more here than meets the eye will probably be the tattooed staff. The young people who work here are covered in ink, some literally from head to toe. They are all former gang members working to find a better path.

The cafe is one of the ventures of Homeboy Industries, a nonprofit started by a local priest, Father Gregory Boyle, on a stated mission to fill "jobs not jails." In the late '80s, Boyle was the leader of Dolores Mission, a Catholic Jesuit parish in East Los Angeles. Gangs dominated the neighborhood, and Father Greg (as he is known) wanted to offer kids an alternative to gang life. In 1988 he created a program called "Jobs For A Future," which eventually became the stand-alone nonprofit Homeboy Industries. In 1992, Boyle launched Homeboy Bakery, where young men learned marketable skills related to making and selling a product.

Over the years Homeboy has expanded its offerings. Their line of chips and salsa is now available at Ralph's supermarkets across the city. And the cafe regularly receives high ratings on Yelp for everything from the pastries to the limeade (called Angela's green potion, its boost of spinach and mint inspires raves).

Without a doubt, the story behind this cafe helps get people in the door the first time. But it's the quality food that turns supporters into regulars.

Address 130 W Bruno Street, Los Angeles, CA 90012, +213.617.0380, www.homeboyindustries.org | **Getting there** US-101 to Alameda Street. Private parking lot. | **Hours** Mon 7am–1:30pm, Tues–Fri 7am–2:30pm, Sat 9am–3pm

52 __ Kools

East meets West

Migration from Japan to the United States began happening in significant numbers following the Meiji Revolution of 1868, which brought widespread social changes. Many Japanese immigrants first settled in Hawaii and San Francisco, and began moving to Los Angeles in the late part of the century for job opportunities and to escape widespread anti-Asian sentiment in the northern part of the state. Following their internment during World War II, Japanese Americans returned to California cities to rebuild the Japantowns they had lost. While it was difficult to reclaim, L.A.'s Little Tokyo once again became a center of Japanese culture, perhaps the best known in the United States.

The best shopping in Little Tokyo is at the Japanese Village Plaza, an outdoor mall that is designed to mimic a traditional village center. There are shops surrounding a small courtyard, all selling items imported from Japan (Hello Kitty and her friends are well represented) or those that Japanese Americans, who come from other parts of the city to eat or shop here, would find interesting (brightly colored sneakers, as well as Shiseido and Shu Uemura cosmetics).

One of the more interesting stores is Kools, which features clothing and accessories inspired by Hot Rod culture, a Japanese-American tradition. Owner Masato Miura, a former drag racer, stocks the shelves with Rat Fink apparel, Japanese tattoo art, and 1950s-inspired dresses, as well as his own line of belts and T-shirts that celebrate motor culture. In a reversal of most of the commerce going on around him, Miura's main business is exporting to Japan. Make sure you check out the remains of the 1923 Ford T Bucket that sits in the middle of the floor. Hot rods were popular among Japanese Americans before the war. Considering the history of the area and the theme of the store, it seems more a monument than a piece of motor history.

Address 110 Japanese Village Plaza Mall, Los Angeles, CA 90012, +1 213.680.1777, www.japanesevillageplaza.net | Getting there US-101 to Los Angeles Street. Parking garage. Or by public transit: Metro train Gold Line to Little Tokyo/Arts District station. | Hours Mon 12pm–6pm, Tues–Fri 12pm–10pm, Sat–Sun 12pm–11pm

53 Larchmont Beauty Center
The most beautiful place in L.A.

There's a very recognizable sound effect that's used in the movies whenever someone encounters their version of paradise. You know it when you hear it: a gospel choir, in unison, exhaling, "Ahhhh." If you love makeup and personal grooming products, I guarantee the chorus will sing the moment you step through the doors at Larchmont Beauty Center.

Owner Sharon Cohanim is unabashedly devoted to creams and the dreams they promise. As her husband, Fred, who oversees the shop day to day, puts it: "She's always doing research." Cohanim is constantly on the hunt for products from around the world that earn high marks from demanding beauty professionals. If it's buzz-worthy, it's shelf-worthy.

Decleor, REN, Molton Brown, Phyto, Mario Badescu, Philip B – you're likely to find them all here, as well as mass-market brands like California Baby, Burt's Bees, Bliss, and L'Occitane. There's also makeup, fragrances, candles – Shiseido, Fresh, Thymes, Tocca, Voluspa – as well as appliances (curling irons, dryers, hot rollers) and tools (makeup brushes, combs, clippers, tweezers). Products are meticulously packed from floor to ceiling in a bright, minimalist presentation. What's more, tucked in the back of the shop is a full-service salon offering hair care, mani/pedis, massage, waxing, and other beauty treatments. So it's possible to have a head-to-toe make-over and leave with everything you need to keep up the look.

No wonder then, that this is the go-to beauty supply outpost for anyone with a stake in the grooming business. Makeup artists, stylists, actors, club kid holdouts, and the "It" girls of every L.A. subculture – they all come here to find that product their friends in Paris, Berlin, London, and Shanghai can't live without. As its website cheekily declares, "If there were a church of cosmetology, Larchmont Beauty Center would be its Vatican."

Address 208 N Larchmont Boulevard, Los Angeles, CA 90004, +1 323.461.0162, www.larchmontbeauty.com, larchmontbeauty@yahoo.com | Getting there I-10 to Western Avenue. Metered street parking. | **Hours** Mon–Sat 8:30am–8pm, Sun 10:30am–6pm

54__ The Last Bookstore

Disneyland for bibliophiles

The Last Bookstore is serious about books – selling new and secondhand volumes that run the spectrum from rare classical literature to pulp to modern masterpieces. They also buy used books from the public, and will accept book donations, which they either sell themselves or give to charity. People pilgrimage here to find beloved titles that they've had a hard time tracking down elsewhere (even online). But the reason locals keep coming back again and again is the epic and eccentric space, capable of inspiring deep reverie and creativity.

The Last Bookstore occupies a 20,000-square-foot former bank, brimming with more than 250,000 volumes. The building, which dates back to 1914, is a historic landmark. In his design of the interior, owner Josh Spencer uses the soaring ornate ceilings, large columns, and former vaults to great effect. Within the majestically cavernous space, tall bookshelves create nooks, with old leather couches sprinkled about.

The second floor of the store is called "The Labyrinth" and has bookshelves arranged in a mazelike configuration. Vaults have been transformed into reading rooms, like the one that holds true crime and mystery books and is decorated to evoke a steampunk hideaway. There's also a domed tunnel lined with books, a yarn shop, and studio spaces where artists create and sell offbeat paintings. Sculptures crop up in corners and overhead, all made with books or inspired by them.

The entire shop feels like an escape, regardless of where it takes you. Just outside, downtown Los Angeles teems with office workers by day and bar patrons by night, and the noise is deafening. But inside, everyone is engaged in quiet pursuit, ensconced in worlds conjured up in books and the magical and madcap environment of the shop. Seeing is believing, and as the Last Bookstore's tagline half-jokingly advises: "What are you waiting for? We won't be here forever."

Address 453 S Spring Street, Los Angeles, CA 90013, +1 213.488.0599, www.lastbookstorela.com, info.lastbookstore@gmail.com | **Getting there** I-110 to Fourth or Sixth Street. Metered street parking. Or by public transit: Metro train Red or Purple Line to Pershing Square. | **Hours** Mon–Thurs 10am–10pm, Fri–Sat 10am–11pm, Sun 10am–9pm

55 The Little Knittery

A yarning passion

Kathleen Coyle doesn't even try to spin a yarn. Well, actually she does. She has been yarn-addicted since her mother taught her to knit when she was eight years old. What Coyle, owner of the Little Knittery, doesn't try to do, is pretend it isn't difficult to sell yarn in sun-kissed Los Angeles. After all, knitting as a craft has had some ups and downs in the last few decades (though it is currently enjoying a resurgence), and while everyone in Southern California owns a sweater or two for chilly nights, Angelenos don't exactly stock up on winter wear each season.

Coyle sells yarn by literally wearing her passion. Before opening the shop, she knits and models her creations and the store is festooned with knitwear and accessories that aren't for sale, but serve as inspiration. Coyle wants her customers to envision what's possible, and it's a strategy that works. Once you walk into this warm, rainbow-colored store you can't leave without believing you are actually capable of knitting something. Good then that the Little Knittery also offers classes for beginners. And Coyle's students are always welcome to return for help with projects (as long as they buy their yarn at the store).

Coyle has always been in the knitting business. She had a long career working as a knitter (creating inspirations) and pattern maker for knitting magazines and for companies that sell knitting products. Her expertise shines through in the yarns she stocks. The Little Knittery only carries natural yarns, many of which are considered luxury or novelty fibers. For example, she has a wide selection of yarns that work well in warm climates, like cotton and lightweight bouclé. Brands like Noro, Berroco, Cascade, Skacel and Ozark Handspun are much more expensive than the acrylics found at craft chains, but the garments made with silk, cashmere, alpaca, and angora will look and feel like a million bucks. No fabrication there!

56 Littlejohn's Candies
The sweet spot

These days, farmers markets are a dime a dozen in L.A., but there can only be one original. The Third Street Market was established in 1934, at the height of the Great Depression, after two entrepreneurs, Fred Beck and Roger Dahlhjelm, proposed "an idea" to turn a plot of prime unused land with great proximity to the growing city into a sellers' "village." Their vision came to fruition that year with farmers, restaurants, and various vendors occupying stalls on the edge of the property. The market was quickly a success, luring Hollywood stars to special events, and becoming a must-visit shopping destination for tourists and locals alike.

The Original Farmers Market continues to be a popular attraction, evolving to accommodate the tastes of the day. In addition to fresh produce, there are meats, fish, cheeses, breads, sweets, pantry items, and prepared foods of all kinds available – from barbecue to vegetarian, Asian to Brazilian, eat-in to takeout. Everyone has their favorite culinary destination but a few of the old-school standouts are Bob's Coffee and Donuts (the apple fritter is killer) and Du-par's, a classic diner and market institution since 1938 (one word: pancakes). But hands down, the sweetest spot has to be Littlejohn's Candies.

Founded in the 1920s by Mr. and Mrs. Littlejohn, the candy company was already enjoying success – their English toffee, in particular, was quite a sensation – when a spot opened up at the farmers market in 1946. The Littlejohns jumped at the opportunity, and in a stroke of brilliance, designed their kitchen with a glass wall so that visitors could watch them make confections like fudge, caramel, and the layered toffee, chocolate, and nuts that had made them famous.

The market's clock tower, erected in the early forties, has become an iconic L.A. landmark. It once stood above an inscription that read: "an idea."

Address 6333 W Third Stall, Stall 432, Los Angeles, CA 90036, +1 323.936.5379, www.littlejohnscandies.com, littljohnscandiesla@yahoo.com | Getting there I-10 to Fairfax. Parking garage. | **Hours** Mon–Fri 9am–9pm, Sat 9am–8pm, Sun 9:30am–7pm

57__Lost & Found

A modern take on the Hollywood strip mall

The strip mall has long been a Los Angeles fixture. Despite their often bleak appearance, you'll sometimes find hidden gems among these clusters of shops and chain stores. Take Sushi Ike in West Hollywood, for example, which has been thrilling foodies for decades from its humble location between a Domino's and a chicken joint. At Lost & Found, the brainchild of owner Jamie Rosenthal, the classic strip mall has been completely re-imagined and elevated to a new, modern, and considerably more upscale level. It all started when Rosenthal, a former stylist, launched a children's store in 2000 that was a hit with the hip mom crowd and decided to expand. Rather than conquering another neighborhood, she simply started stretching out along the block. Today, Lost & Found has grown to include six side-by-side "shops," each with a unique specialty: Children's, Men's, Home, Women's, Gallery, and Gifts.

The operation's headquarters is the gift store, which sells unique artisan products, such as candles from Le Feu de L'eau ("fire of the water"); ballet flats from the venerable French company Repetto; Sans-Arcidet handbags; and colorful pillows and textiles. To browse any of the other stores you need simply ask one of the staff members to let you in. From the children's clothing, which ranges from breezy cotton prints to shrunken hipster-chic sweats, to the home accessories (think hand-woven baskets and rugs), these are the kinds of items a high-end design magazine might feature in a montage of "special finds."

Lost & Found is in an iconic section of Hollywood, but at the turn of the new century the neighborhood didn't have the amenities locals now take for granted, and a high-end children's boutique was an audacious gamble. The store remains somewhat of a hidden treasure, although well known to people in the design and fashion communities, who have made it an essential destination.

Address 6320 Yucca Street, Los Angeles, CA 90028, +1 323.856.5872, www.lostandfoundshop.com, info@lostandfoundshop.com | Getting there US-101 to Vine Street or Hollywood Boulevard. Metered street parking. | Hours Mon–Sat 10am–6pm

58 Louise Green Millinery
If the hat fits

Louise Green has always had a gift for embellishment. She first tried her hand at decorating vintage jackets to sell in consignment shops, but found they didn't do as well as she'd hoped. The few hats she dressed up, however – those flew off the shelves. A British transplant to L.A., Green, who had trained as a fine artist, decided that millinery was her calling and learned the craft from the top hat down.

Louise and her business partner/husband Lawrence have been making and selling vintage-inspired, special occasion hats – for women and men – for three decades now. The store and 9000-square-foot factory are all on the same premises and visitors can peek into the back room to see pork pies, fedoras, cloche hats, and wide brimmed floppies being shaped and stitched and decorated. There are always some 600 to 700 hats in the showroom, all for sale between $200 and $800, and each essentially a custom creation, since everything at Louise Green is handmade.

Customers can also mix and match shapes and trimmings for a hat that is uniquely theirs: felt or straw; a classic band or a bow; silk ribbons, bright flowers, and sparkling crystals; or just a simple feather. Green has also innovated and patented a silk-covered elasticized sweatband that allows the crown of the hat to fit comfortably (even on poofy-hair days).

In the early days of the business, the Greens only sold wholesale, to high-end shops like Saks Fifth Avenue and Neiman Marcus. But people kept knocking on the door and, realizing that there was no other business that's quite like theirs in Los Angeles, they started selling to the public. Today, those-in-the-know, from hipsters to rock stars to mothers of the brides to stylish Derby regulars, come in for a topper that's a crowning glory. Green's artful hats have graced the heads of many a celeb, from Taylor Swift and Gwen Stefani to Shaquille O'Neal and Eva Longoria.

Address 1616 Cotner Avenue, Los Angeles, CA 90025, +1 310.479.1881, www.louisegreen.com, hats@louisegreen.com | **Getting there** I-405 to Santa Monica Boulevard. Street parking nearby. | **Hours** Mon–Fri 9am–4:30pm

59 The Malibu Colony Company

For the person who has everything

It's hard to believe that only twenty years ago there was nowhere in Malibu to find a wide variety of luxury gifts. But according to Tina Nicholls, co-owner of the Malibu Colony Company, that's exactly the void her partner Hugh Kinsella stepped in to fill when he launched the store in 1994.

Malibu Colony, which gets its name from a nearby gated community for the mega rich, stocks furniture, decor, candles, jewelry, fine linens, and unique ornamental items that are too expensive and exquisite to categorize as knickknacks but are definitely more aesthetic than utilitarian. This is where locals go to find a gift for the person who has everything, and it's also good shopping for those who can't spend a fortune but seek something that feels a bit luxe and special. Classics like Baccarat crystal, Buccellati silver, and Faber-Castell pens are stocked alongside more contemporary upscale brands like Dransfield and Ross linens, Diptyque and Voluspa candles, and Arteriors accessories.

The store is nestled into a corner of the Malibu Country Mart, an outdoor mall that has grown around the town's civic center. It's a mixture of boutiques, restaurants, and art galleries that all cater to high-end tastes. The coffee chains Starbucks and Coffee Bean & Tea Leaf are the most proletarian offerings you'll find here. Still, with well-known stores like John Varvatos, M. Fredric, James Perse, and Juicy Couture, as well as a variety of independent shops, the Country Mart is a browser's heaven. It's also a nice stop on a drive up the coast to Santa Barbara, or after a stroll along the famous Malibu pier. And if you have kids in tow, there's a small playground to keep them entertained.

The Malibu Country Mart is also a prime area to spot celebrities, who come here to dine at the satellites of power eateries Nobu and Mr. Chow, or to do a little personal shopping.

Address 3835 Cross Creek Road, Malibu, CA 90263, +1 310.456.7300, www.malibucolonyco.com, info@malibucolonyco.com | Getting there CA-1 to Cross Creek Road. Parking lot. | Hours Mon–Sat 10am–6pm, Sun 12pm–5pm

60 McCabe's Guitar Shop
Get your folk on

Gerald McCabe was a great furniture designer, but there was also no denying that he could fix just about anything made of wood. So when friends of his folk-singing wife started asking him to repair their guitars, he obliged. That was in the 1950s. Today McCabe's is still the place to bring an ailing guitar, or any other stringed instrument, for that matter.

In the intervening years, the store has become iconic among music aficionados, especially those who prefer acoustic sounds. Ry Cooder, who grew up in the area, famously spent his youth hanging out at McCabe's so he could meet great musicians. The store is known for championing quality guitar makers and also has the largest selection of stringed instruments in California, including ukuleles, sitars, latvas, and dulcimers.

McCabe's functions not only as a fabulous shop, but also as a music school. It offers "after school guitar" for kids nine and up. Eighteen-month old "McTots" and kids younger than eight must bring an adult along, so there are several classes that families can enjoy together. But where McCabe's really rocks out is in encouraging folks to get their folk on. There are some classes open to all instruments and others that are specialized. Harmonica players, for instance, can get help with mastering blues bends and warbles, learn Beatles and Stones tunes, and join a music jam. The store even hosts a dulcimer club (where else are you going to meet other devotees?).

McCabe's biggest claim to fame, however, is its back room, which is frequently emptied of instruments and transformed into an intimate concert space featuring unsigned acts as well as world-renowned performers such as Lucinda Williams and Tom Waits. There's no bar but there's always free coffee, which is especially appreciated during their Sunday morning concert series, which presents family-friendly bands from around the country.

Address 3101 Pico Boulevard, Santa Monica, CA 90405, +1 310.828.4497, www.mccabes.com | **Getting there** I-10 to Bundy or Centinela. Metered street parking. | **Hours** Mon–Thurs 10am–10pm, Fri–Sat 10am–6pm, Sun 12pm–6pm

61 Melrose Trading Post

Where future trends meet treasures of the past

Fairfax High School has a storied history in Los Angeles as a pipeline for young Hollywood talent, as well as NFL, NBA, and MLB pros. From classic stars of yesteryear like Carole Lombard and Ricardo Montalban, to Jackson Five brothers Tito and Jermaine, to Demi Moore, Lenny Kravitz, the Red Hot Chili Peppers, and Mila Kunis, the list of the school's celebrity alumni is long and impressive.

Fairfax High is also known for hosting the hippest flea market in the city, Melrose Trading Post (MTP), which occupies its parking lot every Sunday from 9am to 5pm. MTP is strictly for antiques, collectibles, and one-of-a-kind merchandise – such as handmade arts and crafts – so it draws many artisan vendors.

This is ground zero for indie trends because many up-and-coming designers start out here and build a following before opening their own brick-and-mortar. And stylish young Angelenos, eager to be the first to discover the next big thing, make MTP part of their Sunday routine, stopping in before or after brunch. The vintage selection is full of treasures, as well. From a décor-defining 1930s crystal chandelier to a pristine mid-century candy dish, there are great bargains to be had.

The market was started by actors Whitney Weston and Pierson Blaetz, who also founded the Greenway Arts Alliance, a nonprofit that organizes community arts projects. They created MTP as a fund-raiser for the high school and it has been a resounding success, providing support for arts programs as well as professional development for teachers, jobs and internships for students and recent grads, and a host of other benefits.

Fairfax High is located at the tip of the retail strip that's simply known as "Melrose." It has some of the best shopping in Los Angeles, an eclectic mix of boutiques boasting everything from modern street style to designer retro, from sophisticated home decor to kitsch.

Address Fairfax High School, 7850 Melrose Avenue, Los Angeles, CA 90036,
+1 323.655.7679, www.melrosetradingpost.org | Getting there I-10 to Fairfax.
Parking lot. | Hours Sun 9am–5pm; $3 entrance fee

62 Mister Freedom

Bleeding the red, white, and especially the blue

Mr. Freedom is an anti-imperialist satirical cult film from 1969, in which a violently irreverent American superhero, Mr. Freedom, goes to France to take back the country from the communists and ends up destroying it. The premise of the movie inspires a chuckle in the context of Mister Freedom, the menswear store owned by Frenchman Christophe Loiron, who is widely cited as one of the present-day saviors of America's denim heritage.

Loiron moved to Los Angeles in 1990 and became a buyer at American Rag, another vintage institution, before eventually opening Mister Freedom in 2001 to sell his own finds. The store became a destination for the denim obsessed, mainly because Loiron's buys were informed by his deep research on the origins and histories of the items. His process is an inherent assurance of quality and it's not uncommon to hear denim designers list the store as a place they go to for inspiration, and to do their own R & D.

Loiron brings the same attention to his self-made house line – a collaboration with Sugar Cane Co., the celebrated Japanese denim house – which he manufactures in Los Angeles and Tokyo. While the quality of the clothes is undeniable – attention to detail is apparent in the stitch work and embossed leather patches – they don't feel overly "designed." Maybe this is because Loiron goes to great lengths to anchor each line of styles to a particular time and place, even coming up with elaborate backstories for his collections, which have names like "Sea Hunt" (inspired by the French navy's duty to ferret out illegal fishing boats) and "Saigon Cowboy" (a derogatory term for Vietnam-era personnel who ensconced themselves in the city, away from the front line).

The store is arranged in such a way that it's hard to discern what's new and what's "vintage." Which doesn't really matter because it's all undeniably relevant.

Address 7161 Beverly Boulevard, Los Angeles, CA 90036, +1 323.653.2014, www.misterfreedom.com, sales@misterfreedom.com | **Getting there** I-10 to La Brea Avenue. Metered street parking. | **Hours** Daily 11am–6pm

63__ The Mitzvah Store

Good deed shopping

In Hebrew, the word *mitzvah* means "commandment," but this store seems to operate in the spirit of its colloquial meaning – a good or praiseworthy deed. The Mitzvah Store offers Judaica that includes beautiful, artistic Ketubahs, the traditional Jewish marriage contract; engraved silver kiddush cups; shabbat candlesticks; mezuzot; benchers, and other ceremonial items.

The Los Angeles Jewish community is among the most diverse in the United States, with more mixed race and Hispanic Jews than anywhere else in the country. The city also has a significant Persian Jewish population.

The store is owned by Rabbi Shimon Kraft, a community leader known for his work as a scribe of Sefer Torahs and mezuzot. He is usually at the store, happy to answer questions, offer advice, or suggest details for custom items.

The business has two locations, each in a neighborhood with a sizeable number of Jewish residents. The original Pico location is in an area now considered the center of orthodox Jewish life in the city. It is known to non-Jewish Angelenos for its restaurants, including Factor's Famous Deli, which has been a neighborhood institution since 1948 and serves up comforting bowls of matzo ball soup, crispy latkes, hot corned beef on rye, and other Jewish deli favorites. Another landmark, just a few blocks away, is the Museum of Tolerance, the education arm of the internationally renowned Simon Wiesenthal Center, which promotes human rights and is named for the holocaust survivor turned Nazi hunter. Through interactive exhibits and events, the museum teaches visitors about the facts and context of the holocaust and promotes other projects that confront prejudice in all its forms.

Rabbi Kraft also runs a second store, called Mitzvah Too, which is in the hipper Fairfax District.

Address 9400 W Pico Boulevard, Los Angeles, CA 90035, +1 310.247.9613,
www.themitzvahstore.org, info@themitzvahstore.org | Getting there I-10 to
La Cienega Boulevard. Metered street parking. | Hours Mon–Thurs 10am–7pm,
Fri 10am–2pm, Sun 10am–6pm

64 Mohawk General Store

Bringing back the mom-and-pop

The "general store" played an important role in the development of America. During the colonial and post-colonial periods, as Europeans headed west, settling land that would eventually become the United States, they depended on roving peddlers to bring the supplies and materials they would need to permanently establish towns. If these early entrepreneurs found a big enough clientele, they might set up a country or general store to cater to the community. This was especially true for the boomtowns of the California Gold Rush. The country store sold anything and everything, either by stocking it or by acting as middleman. The concept endured for almost two centuries, until the emergence of specialty shops, malls, shopping centers, and all the trappings of modern life made them obsolete.

But in the last few years, the general store has been experiencing a Los Angeles renaissance, with at least a dozen shops prominently embracing the concept. Granted, this isn't the country market of yore, when necessities like grain and fabric were the order of the day. These modern incarnations peddle a combination of items that might include upmarket clothes, fine jewelry, face creams, and artisan crafts and foods.

Mohawk General Store, originally established by husband and wife Kevin and Bo Carney in 2008, is considered a pioneer of the re-imagined one-room department store, selling brand-name labels like Isabel Marant and Issey Miyake, as well as hometown stars like Raquel Allegra's clothing line, Agnes Baddoo bags, and Kathryn Bentley's Dream Collective jewelry line. They also carry apothecary products, textiles, and shoes.

In addition to their flagship store, Mohawk has added two other offshoots: Mohawk Man, just a few doors down, and a second General Store that opened in Pasadena's downtown core. At this rate, the country store will soon become a fixture of city life.

Address 4011 W Sunset Boulevard, Los Angeles, CA 90029, +1 323.669.1601, www.mohawkgeneralstore.com, info@mohawkgeneralstore.com | **Getting there** US-101 to Alvarado Street. Street parking. | **Hours** Mon–Sat 11am–7pm, Sun 11am–6pm

65 Mr. Churro
Deep-fried tradition

The churro, that crispy, chewy fried-dough delight, is also known as the Spanish donut, but at Mr. Churro the influence is definitely Latin American. The Mexican-style churros here are hollow so they can be filled with caramel, cream, chocolate, or strawberry preserves. While the ubiquitous star-shaped variety can be found at vendor carts all over L.A., these stuffed churros, with their crunchy-sweet-sloppy presentation, require a trip to a specialty shop, and Mr. Churro is the best of the bunch.

Undoubtedly the shop benefits from its location on Olvera Street, an outdoor marketplace dedicated to Mexican culture that also serves as a history lesson on the origins of Los Angeles. The street is the site of the oldest home in the city, the Avila Adobe, built in 1818 by Francisco Jose Avila, a Sinaloan Mexican who was mayor of Los Angeles in 1810. The area had become largely neglected by 1926, when a socialite named Christine Sterling launched a campaign to create the street market and save the condemned Adobe, recasting it as a place where American commanders, who won California for the union in the Mexican-American War, had stayed.

A few years later, the exiled Mexican muralist David Alfaro Siqueiros was invited to paint the exterior of a plaza wall. The result was *América Tropical*, a mural that portrayed the country's imperialist treatment of Native and Latin Americans. Not surprising, Sterling didn't approve of the public artwork since it clashed with her plans for the street as a nonpolitical tourist attraction, and within a year the painting was completely covered over.

Since then, Olvera Street has once again reclaimed its place as a center of Mexican culture. The Siqueiros mural was rediscovered, restored, and reopened to the public in 2012. Locals flock to the street to celebrate festivals like Cinco de Mayo and Day of the Dead, and, of course, when only a Mr. Churro churro will do.

Address 12 E Olvera Street, Los Angeles, CA 90012, +1 213.628.1274 | Getting there US-101 to Alameda Street or Broadway. Paid parking lot. | Hours Mon–Thurs 8:30am–7:30pm, Fri–Sun 8:30am–8:30pm

66 Museum of Flying

Preserving California's high-flying legacy

The Museum of Flying Gift Shop at the Santa Monica Airport is designed to satisfy collectors as well as awestruck kids. It's chock-full of air and space memorabilia, like replicas of historic planes and aviators' jackets, and brightly colored aeroprops. More than anything, the shop is meant to provide a lasting souvenir after a couple hours spent hearing stories about the men and women who made this stretch of airstrip historic.

If you've seen *The Aviator* – Martin Scorsese's film about Howard Hughes – you've been introduced to the world that the Museum of Flying preserves. Hughes's drive to create bigger and faster aircraft is prominently acknowledged here. Another figure that looms large is Donald Wills Douglas, who founded the Douglas Aircraft Company (which would become McDonnell Douglas). Douglas and his rival William Boeing made Southern California the aerospace capital of the world during the early 20th century.

In 1974, Douglas's son established a small museum at Santa Monica Airport to display his father's collectibles. However, one important element was missing: there were no planes! That is, until David Price, a local entrepreneur who collected and raced World War II-era planes, donated his collection to the museum for a re-launch in the 1980s. In 2002, the museum fell on hard times and was forced to close down, but 10 years later it took flight again in a new sprawling location on Airport Avenue. Along with the men who inspired its creation, the museum also abounds with the tales of the pioneering women who flew into Santa Monica Airport over the years, including Amelia Earhart, Bessie Coleman, and Sally Ride.

You can pretend to be any of these people as you try out the museum's flight simulator. Or, take a walk across the street to the airport's observation deck to watch the private planes of the Hollywood elite take off into the sunset.

Address 3100 Airport Avenue, Santa Monica, CA 90405, +1 310.398.2500, www.museumofflying.org | Getting there I-10 to Bundy Drive or Centinela Avenue. I-405 to National Boulevard. Private parking lot. | Hours Fri–Sun 10am–5pm

67__Necromance
The art of death

Don't be intimidated by the giant stuffed deer or ostrich in Necromance's shop window that may appear to be giving you the evil eye. Go ahead in. And try not to be daunted by the pierced, tattooed staff who busy themselves keeping everything dusted and meticulously displayed. If you ask them a question, they will answer politely and knowledgeably. For example, you might learn that the skulls, lined up in a case behind labels like "Female Asian" and "1-Year-Old," are in fact resin casts of actual human beings.

This is a shop dedicated to death and dying, but everything is presented with a wink. Sure, there are dead animals. In one half of the store, large trophies of wild game hang overhead, as they would in a fire-lit hunting lodge. But there is also a showcase containing a clutch of adorable fluffy yellow chicks that almost appear to be dancing. The room is flooded with light, and glass-framed butterflies cover most of the wall space.

Owner Nancy Smith is cherubic-looking, with short red hair. The butterflies on the walls are replicated in tattoos along her arms and upper body that look as if they have been merrily sprinkled on. She makes daily trips to estate sales and flea markets to find interesting items to meticulously restore and resell. Why? With a genuine twinkle in her eye, Smith will only say that she has "always liked this kind of stuff." Smith's sense of humor comes shining through in the store's second room, which is filled with whimsical oddities: toy replicas of Wild West guns, a Rexall case full of stylish poison bottles, and surgical instruments that look like they were used in Dr. Jekyll's lair. Even the jewelry pieces Smith stocks continue the death theme, many featuring bones and teeth of small animals.

Necromance is the kind of store your most interesting friend visits to stock up on accessories. When you ask where she gets the stuff, she always pretends she doesn't remember. Now you know.

Address 7220 Melrose Avenue, Los Angeles, CA 90046, +1 323.934.8684,
www.necromance.com | Getting there I-10 to La Brea Avenue. Metered street parking. |
Hours Daily 12pm–7pm

68__Nialaya
Romancing the stone

The story behind this beautiful shop is a gem in itself. On a trip to India, designer Jannik Olander met a shaman named Nialaya, who gave him a reading and then presented him with a black diamond birthstone. Nialaya told Olander that the stone had great powers and advised that he use it wisely. The experience inspired Olander's creation of a line of customizable beaded bracelets that customers can wear as symbols of their inner spiritual life.

Nialaya bracelets are made from silver, gold, and precious stones. For a basic bracelet, which costs between $250 and $350, the wearer is encouraged to choose gems and materials based on the energy and qualities they symbolize and manifest. Cherry quartz, for example, amplifies love and comfort, while brown tigereye is a solid choice if you're looking to achieve insight and confidence. Each bracelet is assembled by hand to ensure that "the energy of the stone supports the bearer in his or her dreams," and is conveniently ready for pickup the next day.

While the company plays up the spiritual aspects and categorizes their creations as "boho luxe," these bracelets are definitely top-shelf status symbols and are frequently seen adorning the wrists of young celebrities. Nialaya's marketing photos feature everyone from Kanye, Beyonce, and Madonna to Bieber, Diddy, and Beckham.

The made-to-order approach allows for bracelets that can run as high as $10,000 or more. Olander sources the stones himself and everything is created in a pristine workshop in the back of the store. Nialaya has also branched out into other jewelry, such as rings and necklaces fashioned from silver, gold, and cubic zirconia.

The luxury prices aside, it's easy to buy into Nialaya's message of inner harmony. Who wouldn't want to bring some peace, love, and understanding wherever they go? For that combination try aquamarine, larimar, and opal.

Address 7922 Melrose Avenue, Los Angeles, CA 90046, +1 310.499.7162,
www.nialaya.com | **Getting there** I-10 to Fairfax Avenue. Metered street parking. |
Hours Mon–Sat 11am–7pm, Sun 12pm–6pm

69__NK Shop

Playing house

Networking is the name of the game in the film and television business, so for many in L.A., a house is not only a home, it's also an event space, a symbol of cool, and a tool to impress potential collaborators. People who are serious about using their homes to express themselves hire an interior designer.

One of young Hollywood's go-to designers is the team of Todd Nickey and Amy Kehoe of the firm Nickey Kehoe. Nickey's background was in retail design and Kehoe's in the hospitality sector before they merged their businesses in 2004 to focus on residential and commercial projects. Named one of the 25 Most Influential Interior Designers in Los Angeles by the entertainment industry's weekly bible, *The Hollywood Reporter*, the duo caters to celebs like actors Ginnifer Goodwin and Mark Ruffalo, and producer Allison Shearmur of the *Bourne* and *Hunger Games* trilogies.

The pair also runs NK Shop, where they sell a variety of their favorite items for the home, which they source from around the globe, including textiles, dishes, unique accessories, and antiques that fit comfortably in modern environments. The merchandise, of course, changes, but what's always on display is the Nickey Kehoe aesthetic, which captures the dichotomy of L.A. chic, where highly designed products are given a lived-in, low-key presentation. Another area of their expertise – and an important aspect of California living – is creating a seamless blend between the indoors and outdoors. The store has two small courtyards that exemplify an integral part of home design for many of the firm's clients.

Nickey Kehoe also has a furniture line, NK Collection, which encompasses their accessible design approach. Even a $7,000 tufted sofa looks like it would make a comfortable spot to curl up with a book. Their NK T Chair appears both ancient and modern, which is exactly the point.

Address 7221 Beverly Boulevard, Los Angeles, CA 90036, +1 323.954.9300,
www.nickeykehoe.com, design@nickeykehoe.com | Getting there I-10 to La Brea
Avenue. Metered street parking. | Hours Mon–Fri 10am–6pm, Sun 10am–5pm

70_ Noodle Stories

Avant-garde fashion for all

Caryl Lee likes to say she's not a fashion person. She opened Noodle Stories when, bags packed and ready to leave Los Angeles, she met someone special who convinced her to stay and she needed to find something to do. That romance is long over, but more than twenty years later, the store, which stocks a bevy of cutting-edge designers, is immensely successful.

So how does a non-fashion person create such a high-fashion experience? By being meticulous. On their buying trips to Paris, Lee and her assistant try on the same styles multiple times, channeling the women who depend on them to choose looks that are on trend but don't make the wearer seem like she's trying too hard. Lee selects avant-garde but accessible designs from lines like Maison Martin Margiela, Commes des Garçons, Y's, and Pleats Please by Issey Miyake, pairing them with Marsell shoes, artistically cut from soft Italian leather, and Luisa Cevese Riedizioni bags, made from a mixture of recycled plastic waste and natural materials.

Noodle Stories caters to accomplished, established women who need to look sharp whether they're at a casual outing or a red-carpet event. As one reviewer succinctly put it, "This is a store for adults." Yes, the clothes are expensive, but they are not intimidating. The pieces Lee stocks from Rei Kawakubo, Junya Watanabe, and the other edgy designers are very approachable. Even the name of the store connotes her unpretentious intentions. "Noodle stories" are silly tales that anyone can tell.

Lee's aesthetic is so consistent and reliable across the board, her loyal clientele has come to rely on her taste season after season. In fact, the shop has so many repeat customers it doesn't even need a sign. So make careful note of the address before you stop by; it's easy to miss the name discreetly noted in the bottom corner of a front window.

Address 8323 W Third Street, Los Angeles, CA 90048, +1 323.651.1782,
www.noodlestories.com, contact@noodlestories.com | Getting there I-10 to La Cienega
Boulevard. Metered street parking | **Hours** Mon–Sat 10am–6pm, Sun 12pm–5pm

71_Oasis Imports
Where worlds collide

Driving up the Pacific Coast Highway (or PCH as the locals call it) on the way to Malibu, you'll notice an abundance of furniture that seems to be creeping onto the street. That's Oasis Imports, and you should always stop at an oasis.

The roadside emporium is owned by David Haid, and once you hear his story, this store makes perfect sense. Twenty-plus years ago, Haid went to Tonga on a family vacation, and ended up staying for more than a year. During that time he got a job on a sailboat and became enamored with the many handicrafts he encountered on his travels through the Asia-Pacific region. He returned to Los Angeles in search of the perfect corner to open a shop to sell his finds, finally settling into this iconic stretch of PCH where the seaside lifestyle of Malibu and the hippie vibes of Topanga Canyon happily coalesce.

Oasis has an eclectic array of beautiful all-weather furniture, as well as indoor and outdoor accessories. Ceramic pots from Mexico, painted Moroccan tiles, gilded tables from India, and beautifully painted Italian shade umbrellas join a variety of gifts that are probably easiest to describe as knickknacks (a mermaid made of a coconut shell, painted ceramic skulls, a piece of African mud cloth). Haphazardly hung on the walls are beachy-looking signs, with phrases like Touch Me, that Haid custom-creates. The result is that Oasis feels like a stylish bazaar filled with the types of treasures you never knew you wanted but somehow can't resist.

Haid travels to a new location every so often – China, Italy, India, Mexico, or Africa – and stays long enough to explore and fill a shipping container. He buys directly from artisans because that model enables his philosophy for the store: "The best best best the world has to offer, for the least least least." The items cover the gamut in prices, but Haid loves haggling, so there's always a deal to be had.

Address 3931 Topanga Canyon Boulevard, Malibu, CA 90265, +1 310.456.9883, www.oasisimports.com, daveatoasis@hotmail.com | **Getting there** CA-1 to Topanga Canyon Boulevard. Private parking lot. | **Hours** Daily 10am–6pm

72_ The Original Los Angeles Flower Market

Bargain blooms

Among the citrus groves that dominated the Southern California landscape two centuries ago, flower farms also began popping up as newly arrived Japanese immigrants started planting fields in the Santa Monica area. By the beginning of the 20th century, the floral industry was booming and wholesalers began opening businesses downtown – among them the Southern California Flower Market, established by Japanese growers, and the Los Angeles Flower Market.

Anchored by these two markets, which are located across the street from each other and surrounded by dozens of small merchants, L.A.'s flower district is the largest in the country. While there are deals to be had throughout the area, the Original Los Angeles Flower Market, with fifty different vendors and an amazing variety of buds and price points, is the most popular – especially with the public. You see, the flower district mainly caters to wholesalers. This is where the event planners, decorators, and boutique florists come to stock up – and the predawn hours are reserved for these professionals. But at either 6am or 8am, depending on the day, the market opens up to the public.

From not-so-fresh arrangements on clearance for $1 to a massive bushel of roses for $25, the Original Los Angeles Flower Market makes it easy to have a house full of fresh blooms for about what it would cost for one bouquet from the corner grocery. The vendors here also sell all the accessories you need to complement your flowers – vases, foam blocks, wire ribbons, etc. But don't expect the same kind of fancy packaging you find at a flower shop. Market sellers generally quick wrap your bouquets in sheets of newspaper.

The entrance fee runs $1 or $2 depending on the time and day of the week. Parking downtown is expensive and the market has a rooftop parking structure. It's not free, but it costs about the same as a meter.

73__Pamper & Play
The answer to a parent's prayers

Every overextended parent knows the frustration of having a baby-sitter bail at the last moment or of trying to sneak in some multitasking only to realize, a couple minutes later, that their child has been up to some tasks of his or her own. Creative designer Carol Cablk and her husband are parents of two young boys. Both used to work from home and occasionally faced one of those inevitable scenarios. Cablk dreamed of a place "where I could drop in and relax or get some work done while my kids had a blast!" When she couldn't find such a place, she decided to create it herself.

Think of Pamper and Play as a time out (the good kind) for kids – and for their parents. Unlike most indoor play spaces, where parents must keep a close eye on the action to make sure no bones are broken, at Pamper and Play, adults are invited to take the stairs up from the play floor to a comfy loft area that has been converted into a sitting room. There, they can relax, read a book, or get all those work tasks completed while a staff of trained pros watches their little ones. Coffee, tea, and Wi-Fi are complimentary.

Downstairs, the kids can roll around in ball pits, climb, play dress up or house, or enjoy a story, all under the watchful eyes of background-checked, CPR-certified "play supervisors." And parents who are having some separation anxiety can easily sneak a peek at the fun. For toddlers who are fast approaching pre-school, this also doubles as a stress-free way to practice drop-off.

If you're really in a bind and must leave your child, Pamper & Play offers another innovative program: their Create-a-Camp option. While one child is enough to secure the service, the more who sign up, the cheaper it gets. And every weekend there's Parents' Time Out, a four-hour drop-off where kids play and eat pizza while parents work, run errands, or enjoy some well-earned peace and quiet. No multitasking necessary.

CHILDREN HOLD THEIR PARENTS' HANDS FOR A SHORT TIME, BUT HOLD THEIR HEARTS FOREVER

Address 2279 Westwood Boulevard, Los Angeles, CA 90064, +1 310.441.0797, www.pamperplay.com | Getting there I-10 to Overland Avenue. Metered street parking. | Hours Mon–Fri 10am–5pm, reservations for weekend

74_ Panpipes Magickal Marketplace

A witchy take on life

When Vicky Adams was a kid growing up in Australia, she read the entire *World Book Encyclopedia* for fun. The payoff came when she got to the Ws and discovered the history of witchcraft, which sparked the beginning of a lifelong fascination with the occult. Adams went on to become a graphic designer, but while on a visit to the United States in 1997, she kept hearing about a magical shop in Hollywood that everyone said she would love. And that's how Adams discovered Panpipes, the store she'd one day own.

Panpipes bills itself as the nation's oldest occult retailer. Its roots date back to the Weird Museum of Hollywood, a tourist attraction that opened in 1961 and claimed to house the bones of Vlad the Impaler, also known as Vlad Dracula, whose name inspired Bram Stoker's famous vampire. The store cycled through a couple other names (and locations) before settling on Panpipes. In 1995, it was bought by the actress Fairuza Balk, whose film about teenage witches, *The Craft*, was about to hit theaters. Adams started working for Balk, and eventually took over ownership of the shop.

Adams uses alchemical concepts to create candles, mojo, or gris-gris bags containing amulets or stones for customers in search of specific outcomes, such as financial success, love, or professional advancement. The store is also an apothecary, and Adams mixes essential oils and herbs to make one-of-a-kind scents that are created with a particular purpose in mind. For first-time clients, Adams will ask several questions before recommending and preparing a talisman, candle, or perfume.

Adams has devotees who come from near and far to seek her advice. The shop can get pretty crowded, but don't be dissuaded – it only takes a few minutes to have a consultation, and there are many items to browse while you wait to see the witchiest woman in the West.

Address 1641 N Cahuenga Boulevard, Los Angeles, CA 90028, +1 323.462.7078, www.panpipes.com | Getting there US-101 to Cahuenga Boulevard. Metered street parking. | Hours Tues–Fri 11am–6pm, Sat 10am–6pm

75_Phoenix Imports
One dress fits all

The *cheongsam* or *qipao* is the traditional high-necked, floral Chinese dress that has been around since the 17th century. Originally made of silk with intricate embroidery and a long skirt and sleeves, the dress evolved into the style that's well known today, featuring a body-hugging skirt, side slit, and cap sleeves. One can find a range of designs, from the classic versions seen at formal weddings to the much cheaper printed polyester varieties worn by hostesses at Chinese restaurants.

Regardless, the *cheongsam* looks stylishly elegant and beautiful on women of all sizes and races. While Phoenix Imports sells an array of gift items, if you've ever wanted to add a *cheongsam* to your wardrobe (and you should), this is the place to score one for a price that won't break the bank. The cost of each dress is based on the material and whether it's the garden variety or a vintage version.

The shop is located in the Central Plaza of Los Angeles's Chinatown. Step into this courtyard lined with businesses, and you'll be swept away to a different time. Chinese immigrants were first documented in the mid-19th century and this plaza, dedicated in 1938, is considered the epicenter of one of the United States' first modern Chinatowns.

The shops are a mix of the old and the new, from social clubs where retirees congregate to hip establishments like Ooga Booga, which carries high-end art, books, and clothing. This is also a gathering place for the Chinese New Year celebration, especially for the annual Golden Dragon Parade, which has been a tradition for more than 100 years and includes dozens of floats and marching bands in addition to the customary dragon dances and festive lanterns. Since 2013, the plaza has also been home to a seven-foot bronze statue of legendary actor Bruce Lee, who brought martial arts to the mainstream and died when he was only 32 years old.

Address 463 Gin Ling Way, Los Angeles, CA 90012, +1 213.680.9640 | Getting there I-110 to Hill Street. Metered street parking. | Hours Daily 12pm–8pm

76__Plastica

Pretty polymers

In 1967's *The Graduate*, Dustin Hoffman's Benjamin Braddock received one word of advice from his parents' friend: "Plastics!" The '60s were the decade when the polymers first started appearing in the utilitarian applications we take for granted today. Plastica's owner Carla Denker could well have gotten the same directive. Although the shop has evolved to include a wider definition of the plastic arts, which Denker describes as "ceramic, sculptural, and beyond," it started out in 1996 as her quest to find and bring unusual plastic goods to L.A.'s curious shoppers. Her first hit was a collection of woven market bags from Mexico. And then, she met Rody.

Developed in Italy in 1984, Rody is a plastic jumping horse that has caught on like wildfire with Los Angeles toddlers over the last 15 years. The smiling bouncy horse comes in a rainbow of colors and is a fixture in playrooms and child care centers. Plastica may have been the first store in L.A. to carry Rody, as Denker has been stocking the toy since at least 1999.

The shop doesn't just sell plastics, although the basic meaning of the word, "pliable or moldable," would apply to a lot of the interesting products amassed here. There are also fabric goods, like tote bags bearing the California map, beautiful dishes and cutlery made from bamboo, leather bags, and jewelry. Still, the most interesting thing about Plastica is that it makes you realize that despite the bad rap plastic has garnered in environmental circles, it brings us great, sculptural beauty: graphic rugs made from recycled polypropylene, a melamine bread box that doubles as a cutting board, a slender jug with a screw cap that keeps liquids hot for five hours, a sailing-ship kite made from nylon and Balinese bamboo – even lenticular postcards featuring images from nature or the Los Angeles skyline. All great examples of plastic's versatility and sleek aesthetic potential.

77_Primo's Donuts

Made fresh daily, since 1956

Hands down, Primo's sells the best donut in Los Angeles. And their secret is pretty simple: they make everything fresh each morning. As owner Ralph Primo says, "there's never a day-old donut at Primo's."

Ralph, 84, and his wife, Celia, 81, have been in the donut business since 1956, when Ralph Jr., then three years old, spied a donut shop and started to beg: "Donut! Donut!" It had been a hard morning. The Primos had finally managed to raise $500 as the down payment for a Culver City house (that was a lot of money back then) only to have it rejected by the seller. Ralph, hoping to build up their savings, asked the owner of the shop if he was looking for help. The man had only been open for six months, and confessed he was already going under and needed to sell. Ralph offered to buy the place on the spot, convincing the shop owner to give him two days to raise the $2000 asking price.

The plan – at least as he explained it to a stunned but supportive Celia – was to build the business up for a year, then sell at a profit. As Ralph puts it now, "Sometimes it helps to be young and stupid." It took about three more years than expected, but Primo's Donuts did become a success. By then Ralph and Celia were too deeply in love with donuts to give up the store.

In the intervening years there have been some changes. The neighborhood has transitioned from mostly corn and celery fields to freeways and strip malls. And a donut today costs $1.25, not the 5¢ it did in '56. But much also remains the same. The perennial favorite flavor is still buttermilk (although bacon usually sells out faster); Ralph and Celia still spend the wee hours of every morning whipping up dozens of donuts; and the regulars still come in to gripe about the Lakers (who aren't even as old an L.A. tradition as Primo's), with their children, grandchildren, and even great-grandchildren in tow.

Address 2918 Sawtelle Boulevard, Los Angeles, CA 90064, +1 310.478.6930, www.primosdonuts.com | Getting there I-10 to Overland Avenue. I-405 to National Boulevard. Private parking lot. | Hours Mon–Fri 5:30am–4pm, Sat 6am–3pm, Sun 7am–1pm

78_Queen Mary

Ship shopping

Long Beach is the hometown of Snoop Dogg and Cameron Diaz (they knew each other in high school). It's also the last beach community before Los Angeles yields to Orange County. The beaches here are popular with families because a breakwater keeps high waves from crashing into the shore, which precludes great surfing but makes for pleasant swimming. There are also many other aquatic activities, including kayaking, kite and windsurfing, and sailing, as well as waterfront attractions to lure people to the shore. Primary among them is the *Queen Mary*.

The *Queen Mary* has a history worthy of her royal name. Her first voyage, from Southampton, England, was in 1936, and for three years afterward she held the title of the fastest transatlantic ocean liner. The ship was frequented by celebrities and dignitaries like Bob Hope and Winston Churchill. During the Second World War she was a troopship, then once again became a luxury liner in 1947. She sailed for 20 more years before retiring to Long Beach. These days the great old dame is a floating hotel and event venue with world-class restaurants and – although it doesn't receive top billing – great shopping.

The *Queen Mary's* retailers run the gamut. There's Stacks Gift Shop, which sells souvenirs like mugs and T-shirts; the Princess Diana shop, a complement to the ship's "Diana: Legacy of a Princess" exhibition, which includes gowns, accessories, and personal memorabilia; and Malibu Family Wines, the local producer of Semler and Saddlerock wines; as well as boutiques selling apparel and accessories. There's also a day spa offering facials, massage, and other pampering services.

Climbing aboard the *Queen Mary* requires either a ticket to a tour or exhibition or the purchase of a $15 food voucher. If you just want to head for the shops, go for the voucher, which can be applied to any bill at the ship's restaurants and lounges.

Address 1126 Queens Highway, Long Beach, CA 90802, +1 562.499.1759, www.queenmary.com | **Getting there** I-710 to Queen Mary. Parking garage. | **Hours** Varies by store

79 __ Rastawear Collection
Ode to red, gold, and green

When Bob Marley brought reggae to the world in the 1970s, he also brought his Rastafari religion and its emblematic colors: red, gold, and green. The Jamaican singer died in 1981, but remains one of the best-selling artists around the globe, with a devoted cult-like following.

As Marley's legacy endures, so does the popularity of Rasta colors. They are worn by his fans, reggae music buffs, proponents of marijuana legalization (Rastas consider cannabis their sacrament), and those who love Jamaica, where the Rastafarian movement originated.

On Venice Beach, L.A. headquarters for all things counterculture, it's easy to find clothing and accessories boasting the red, gold, and green. When Jamaican-born stuntman Don Salmon first moved to L.A., he noticed the glut, but also realized that the cultural significance wasn't being recognized, and hatched a plan to open an authentic Rasta store. At Rastawear Collection, Salmon carries lines endorsed by the Marley family, including *Catch A Fire*, designed by Marley's daughter Cedella. Salmon also designs for the store himself, mostly applying the Rasta aesthetic to popular fashion trends.

The Rastawear Collection store is located in a mini promenade of unique retail shops called Gingerbread Court, which is accessed from Venice's main boardwalk. What distinguishes Salmon's boutique from the $5 knockoffs being sold in the beach's ramshackle stalls is the high quality of the clothing and accessories, including bags, hats (everything from beanies to fedoras), and even pet collars.

In addition to the surf and sand, people come to Venice to experience the wacky creativity of performers and artists who line the boardwalk. The Venice Beach Freakshow, which features two-headed turtles, fire-eaters, and a bearded lady is emblematic of the vibe. And after they've had their fill, visitors realize there's some great shopping to be done.

Address 517 Ocean Front Walk, Suite 2, Venice, CA 90291, +310.399.2371, www.rastawearcollection.com | Getting there I-405 to Venice Boulevard. Beach parking. | Hours Daily 10am–7:30pm

80_ Reddi Chick

Chicken and fries with staying power

Reddi Chick is one of only three stores that have occupied spaces at the Brentwood Country Mart since it opened in 1948. Its fans drive from all over the city for its signature rotisserie chicken, which can be ordered whole or in pieces, and many argue their fries are also the best around. Plus, Reddi Chick's simple basket of meat and potatoes is probably the only thing about the Brentwood Country Mart that actually still feels country.

Not that there was ever anything simplistic about the Mart. It was conceived as a West Side version of the city's Original Farmers Market (see p. 120), which now shares its identity with the Grove shopping mall on Fairfax. Both markets were designed in the style of British and early American marketplaces, with barn-inspired facades and a center courtyard that is ringed by shops selling everything from culinary staples to imports. And this being Brentwood, a neighborhood that's long been favored by Hollywood types, the Mart's original marketing plan employed celebrities to patronize the shops and attend events like fashion shows, exhibits, and community fund-raisers. It soon became a reliable venue for star-spotting, and the resulting crowds fueled its success.

These days the crowds come for the chicken. The menu's BBQ birds and ribs also are popular. Reddi Chick and the other thriving food vendors that line the Country Mart courtyard make it a busy weekday lunchtime destination, especially during the months when the large fire pit at its center is lit, evidence that yes, L.A. does have seasons!

The retail stores cater to the high-end tastes of fickle fashionistas, and thus popularity grows and wanes. But Reddi Chick never goes out of style, and celebrity sightings are still a regular occurrence here. They too drop by on their way home to grab some rotisserie for a favorite family dinner.

Address 225 26th Street, Santa Monica, CA 90402, +1 310.393.5238,
www.brentwoodcountrymart.com | **Getting there** I-10 to Cloverfield Boulevard. I-405 to
Wilshire Boulevard. Private parking lot. | **Hours** Mon–Sat 10am–8pm, Sun 11am–7pm

81 Requisite

A Beverly Hills spin on Savile Row

Angeleno Jeric Rivera graduated from college with a degree in marketing and design but didn't relish the prospect of a career that involved creating knockoff knickknacks for global chains. Since those were the types of jobs he was finding, he opted instead for an apprenticeship with a master tailor. A suit he made for a local bartender led to word-of-mouth business that reached all the way to the top echelons of a major studio. Now everyone – from film execs to actors, directors, and international models – flocks to Rivera and his partner, Lauren Gold, for Hollywood's take on bespoke.

Requisite certainly harkens back to the made-to-measure approach of Savile Row. Every suit is developed from scratch using the finest materials available. While they keep business hours, visits to their Beverly Hills fitting studio are by appointment only, and there's no signage announcing the location because it might encourage passersby to wander in.

But unlike the custom tailors of yore, Rivera and Gold prefer a more renegade approach, acting as therapists, stylists, and designers in outfitting their clients. Who says you can't have ankle-length pants, wear your trousers on your hip, or use offbeat prints? As Rivera puts it: "There's no right or wrong, just preference."

Requisite offers free consultations. They don't use look-books or samples, preferring to partner with each client to create something original. It's then on to choosing materials, everything from your traditional fabrics to vicuña wool or a unique pattern. The process can take weeks or months, depending on details and whether the client is decisive. And while price is commensurate, it ranges on average between $900 and $1,500.

Rivera once made a $15,000 suit that required the manufacture of a specially designed fabric. He and Gold relish these types of demanding requests. It keeps their job fresh, fun, and creatively challenging.

Address 140 S Beverly Drive, Suite 205, Beverly Hills, CA 90212, +1 800.617.6313, www.requisiteclothing.com, info@requisiteclothing.com | Getting there I-10 to Robertson Boulevard. Metered street parking. | Hours By appointment only

82__Robinson Beautilities

Rent a transformation

No one seems to know for sure who gave Robinson Beautilties its supercalifragilistic name, just that it started life as a beauty supply store and presumably someone named Robinson was involved. Today, it's the largest costume rental store in Los Angeles, stocked with all sorts of elaborate getups – ballroom gowns, flapper dresses, and gold lamé galore. There's everything you need to pretend you've signed up for the military, stepped into an old Western, or even joined the gang on Sesame Street. The store is a kooky hodgepodge of costume racks, a makeup and wig studio, and, inexplicably, a mini pinball arcade, which one can surmise is either there to entertain waiting customers or as an additional source of revenue in the quieter months between December and September.

Robinson Beautilities rose to popularity in the '80s and '90s, in the days before pop-up Halloween stores became the rage. Back then it was one of the only places you could get an authentic getup, whether you wanted to be a French maid, a Vegas showgirl, or a local mascot, like USC's Tommy Trojan. And in the final days leading up to October 31st, lines would trail out the door and down the street, and passing traffic would slow to a crawl as desperate last-minute shoppers tried to find parking. This was also "the" place to go when Hollywood stars were throwing costume parties or the Playboy Mansion was hosting a themed event.

Even though it's no longer the only show in town, the shop remains an L.A. institution. Rental outfits, which can be had for between $50 and $75, are stuffed in from floor to ceiling, and you get the distinct feeling that this is the kind of place where items are added but never subtracted. Which makes sense, since many are one-of-a-kind creations, sourced from Hollywood productions.

Whoever Robinson was or is, thanks is owed for bringing beautilities to the people.

83_Rose Bowl Flea Market
The lord of the fleas

No doubt about it, this is the granddaddy of West Coast flea markets. Housed at the world-famous stadium that has hosted Olympic events, World Cup matches, and a few Super Bowl championships, it is the preferred market for design professionals and the celebrities they work for. The once-a-month Rose Bowl Flea happens on the second Sunday, features 2500 vendors, attracts 20,000 shoppers, and offers a tiered entry fee that separates the genuine buyers from the looky-loos.

There is nothing you need that you won't find for sale here – high-end furniture, jewelry, clothing, art, housewares, toys, books, music; new, vintage, or antique. The stadium has a capacity of more than 90,000, so there's a lot of ground to cover, which is why you should also wear comfortable shoes, stay hydrated, and – this being Southern California – come armed with sunscreen and a fashionable brimmed hat.

People-watching here is great fun. There are many colorful characters among the most serious collectors and resellers, some who hail from as far away as Japan and Europe, and of course there are bound to be a few celebrities to be glimpsed, not to mention the beautiful and stylish Hollywood hoi polloi.

It's wise to at least empty your trunk beforehand (though if you can borrow a bigger vehicle, do so; it's just smart planning). More and more vendors are starting to take credit cards, but cash is king if you plan to haggle, and you should – everything at the market is priced for negotiation. All except the admission fee, that is, which serial "Bowlers" say is well worth it. This hardcore bunch usually pays $20 for the predawn VIP preview, from 5am to 7am, with flashlights in hand. Early entry, from 7am to 8am, is $15, from 8am to 9am is $10, and from 9am onward is $8. The fair wraps up by 4:30pm but many vendors are ready to pack it in beginning at around 3pm. That's when the real bargains are made.

Address 1001 Rose Bowl Drive, Pasadena, CA 91103, +1 323.560.7469, www.rgcshows.com | **Getting there** I-210 to Berkshire, Lincoln Avenue / Washington Boulevard or Arroyo / Windsor; SR 134 to Linda Vista / San Rafael. Private parking lot. | **Hours** Second Sunday of every month, 5am–4:30pm

84_ Roseark

Inspired by nature

Every three months, Roseark unveils an exhibition by an artist or jewelry designer in its back room. A recent show featured painter Laura Ball, whose ethereal watercolors are a celebration of nature, which is perfectly in tune with the jewelry that Kathy Rose designs for the store she owns with her former husband and business partner, Rick Rose.

Rose's line, which ranges in price from a few hundred dollars to upwards of $10,000, is largely inspired by fauna and flora. She made her name with a cuff that looks like a coiling snake. A diamond bracelet inspired by an antelope and matching ring, a signature dozen-roses necklace, and a manta ray pendant carved from bone, ebony, or mother-of-pearl are other striking examples of her work. Her minimalist sideways cross necklace has adorned many a celebrity clavicle, including Rihanna, Jennifer Lopez, Miley Cyrus, and Kourtney Kardashian. Rose is also known for creating custom engagement rings, and she offers both original designs or enhanced family heirlooms.

Roseark sells jewelry from more than 40 other designers, as well. Standouts include Thorn drop earrings by Elisabeth Bell, 14K gold Spirit Animal necklaces by Carmen Diaz, and bezel-set eternity-style stackable rings by Sethi Couture.

The Roseark boutique is itself part of the pleasure of the shopping experience. It's tucked into the corner of two busy intersections in hip West Hollywood, behind a perfectly trimmed hedge with the store's name floating above the bright green foliage. Ring the bell to be let into a neat little garden and up a short flight of stairs. The beautifully curated shop feels like a chic friend's professionally decorated cottage. Each room is exquisitely ornamented with jewelry, art, and other treasures for sale. Rose's well-heeled regulars visit the store by appointment, but you're welcome to buzz if you just happen to be in the neighborhood.

Address 1111 N Crescent Heights Boulevard, West Hollywood, CA 90046, +1 323.822.3600, www.roseark.com | Getting there US-101 north to Santa Monica Boulevard. Metered street parking. | Hours Mon–Fri 11am–6pm; advance appointment recommended

85__Route 66 Modern Classics

Get your kickstands

The Route 66 scooter store is located next door to Bartels' Harley-Davidson, one of California's largest dealers of the iconic brand's motorcycles and accessories. But it's not the David vs. Goliath scenario you might imagine. Route 66 is owned by Glenn Bartels, whose parents started the Harley superstore. In 1994, Glenn clued in on the demand for Harley rentals (his parents' shop doesn't offer this service) and started Route 66 as a place to rent a hog and hit the open road.

The Harley rentals were a huge success, but Glenn quickly noticed that another kind of motorcycle was also rising in popularity in Southern California's beach communities – the scooter. So Route 66 started selling, renting, and repairing these sleek, brightly colored bikes. The store is a dealer of the Taiwanese-built Buddy line, and sells and repairs used Vespas, the Italian brand that pioneered the motorbike's design. The high demand for scooters in Los Angeles correlates with the fact that gas prices in California are frequently among the highest in the nation. Scooters are fuel efficient and with their step-through design, which allows the rider to firmly plant both feet on the floorboard, they're also easy to operate. Whenever the cost of gas soars, so do scooter sales.

At Route 66 you can try out a scooter before committing. Rentals are $66 per day for a week or less, and go down to $49 for longer than seven days. They also sell motorcycles by Royal Enfield, makers of the classic design known as the "Enfield Indian," which was developed and manufactured in India in the 1950s.

But when it comes to motorcycles, Harleys are still the king of the road. Between April and October, when the weather is super nice, it costs $225 to take a Harley out for 24 hours. In the off-season the price goes down to $185.

Address 4161 Lincoln Boulevard, Marina Del Rey, CA 90292, +1 310.578.0112, www.rt66mc.com, rt66mc@gmail.com | **Getting there** CA-90 West to Lincoln Boulevard. Private parking lot. | **Hours** Tues–Sat 10am–6pm, Sun 10am–5pm

86__Rumba

Make yourself at home

One might hesitate before stepping into Rumba because the exquisitely designed furniture shop looks intimate enough to be someone's house. Perhaps that's because it is. Rumba is the store, studio, showroom, and home of Kimba Hills, who designs furniture as well as interiors. The living room in the store window – that's her living room. And she's been known to patter out in her pajamas to rearrange furniture. At the back of the house / store, are her kitchen, bedroom, and dining room. It's all decorated in Hills's modern European-inspired aesthetic. And everything, including her style, is for sale. "I have to order a new headboard because I just sold the one I had," she says, quickly adding, "We custom-make the headboards ourselves."

Hills also carries refurbished vintage furniture and showcases local artists, whose paintings decorate the walls. The paintings, like all the other pieces, are available for purchase. Hills adopted her here-today-gone-tomorrow approach from her previous career as a production designer. She enjoyed the process of creating interiors for films and television shows, only to watch everything be carted off before beginning afresh on a new design. The same thing happens at her store and she claims to not be attached to anything that's out in the open. That beautiful wine rack made of corrugated cardboard nestling two unopened bottles in her kitchen? Yes, that could be yours for a price. Hills's large right-angled couch is perhaps the biggest mover in the place. She designed it as the answer to many a client's wish list: firm but not too hard, big but with clean lines, able to accommodate people and pillows. It can be produced within two weeks for $7,500 and shipped anywhere.

There is one room that's off-limits to shoppers – her son's bedroom. He's off to college now after writing a well-received application essay about what it's like to grow up in a showroom.

Address 1740 Ocean Park Boulevard, Santa Monica, CA 90405, +1 310.392.3103,
www.kimbahills.com, info@kimbahills.com | Getting there 1-10 to Cloverfield Boulevard
or 20th Street. Metered street parking. Or by public transit: Big Blue Bus Route 8 to
17th Street. | Hours Tues–Fri 10am–6pm, Sat 11am–5pm, Mon by appointment

87__Rust

Wear your emotions in your hair

Rust is a hair salon. And they do all the things you'd expect at a typical salon – cuts, blowouts, highlights, etc. But they also create RustLocks, where a lock of hair is transformed into a jeweled expression of the wearer's personality. Clients can bring in crystals, stones, beads, jewelry, rocks, arrowheads, or anything else that's meaningful in their lives, as long as it can be adhered to yarn. Rust stylists wrap a lock of hair, incorporating the items to create an accessory that's unique, individualized, and illustrates the wearer's personal story. "That coin? I found it in a bazaar in Morocco, and this is a ring my mother gave me when I turned sixteen."

RustLocks are the brainchild of the shop's founder, Tara Tatangelo. A makeup artist and hair stylist who likes to work with clients who don't mind standing out, she counts rockers like Travis Barker and Slash among her clients and can do killer ombres in any trendy color (hello, purple!).

For clients who want a lock that's deeply personalized, Tatangelo will do a consultation and suggest items based on how their meanings correspond with the wearer's aspirations, using charms, color theory, astrology, or just her discerning eye. The resulting custom creation can take an hour or two to make and will cost between $50 and $200, depending on the length and items used. The wrap is sewn onto the client's hair to keep it in place so it can be worn for years.

RustLocks resemble the funkiest dreadlocks ever, so this is also about having a fierce, fun look. It's not surprising that Tatangelo has taken her RustLocks craftiness to Burning Man, the annual festival in the Nevada desert that's dedicated to self-expression.

For clients who don't live in Los Angeles, Rust creates clip-on RustLocks. Just mail them your emotion-heavy trinkets or have them surprise you with something that's one-of-a-kind.

88 __ Saffron & Rose Ice Cream

A parlor of international flavors

A double scoop: one of saffron pistachio, the other white rose. Remember that. It's the signature order at this ice-cream shop in the heart of Tehrangeles, the part of Westwood Boulevard that is known for its many Iranian businesses. And this is one of the most popular shops among Persians who come to Westwood to shop or meet friends for a meal.

Iranian ice cream is made from whole milk, which makes it thicker and richer than standard American fare. Chunks of clotted cream, mixed in to provide texture, might be startling to unaccustomed palates but give each bite an extra creamy boost.

Other standout scoops include lavender and ginger, and there is always an assortment of fruity sorbets. The attendants will supply tasting spoons, so be sure to try the refreshing cucumber flavor, which has bits of julienned cucumber mixed in. Standard flavors like chocolate and vanilla are on the menu as well, but don't hold up the line for those.

There are two other treats you may not recognize but must sample. *Faloodeh* is made from small, extra-thin vermicelli noodles that have been frozen in rosewater syrup. *Ice in Heaven* is a well-known Iranian custard ice made from starch and milk, but here they add chia seeds, which seems like a decidedly L.A. touch. Both desserts are topped with lemon and sour-cherry syrup, which sit in squeeze bottles at the end of the counter so customers can help themselves to as much as they'd like. Persians often make ice-cream sandwiches using thin, crispy wafers, and those are available here too.

Saffron and Rose isn't the kind of ice-cream parlor where you take the kids to while away a couple hours. It's small and cramped and the seating is no-frills. Even Iranian regulars don't stay long. The shop has its most popular flavors packed in to-go cups (bearing a striking image of its late founder) and provides cold packs that will travel for up to an hour and a half.

Address 1387 Westwood Boulevard, Los Angeles, CA 90024, +310.477.5533, www.golobolbol.org | **Getting there** I-405 North to Santa Monica Boulevard or Wilshire Boulevard. Metered street parking. | **Hours** Sun–Thurs 8am–10:30pm, Fri–Sat 8am–11pm

89 Santa Monica Jewelry & Loan
The anti-pawnshop

Yes, Santa Monica Jewelry and Loan is a pawnshop. They hold your personal effects for a designated period of time in exchange for "loans" from "$5 to $1 million." But Santa Monica Jewelry and Loan doesn't act, or look, like a typical pawnshop. For one thing, the customer service is superior. The staff greets you as if you're walking into the fine jewelry department of a trendy store. Which, come to think of it, you essentially are. The interior is set up in a bright minimalist style, with jewelry along one side and vintage guitars – which the store has a reputation for stocking – on the other.

Santa Monica Jewelry and Loan is located in the heart of the seaside downtown, just steps away from the swanky Santa Monica Place mall, full of high-priced boutiques like Tory Burch, Michael Kors, Tiffany & Co., and Ben Bridge Jewelers. Moreover, the shopping center sits at the south end of the Third Street Promenade, a three-block stretch of popular retailers.

All these stores are competition. Santa Monica Jewelry and Loan sells the same quality products they do: David Yurman earrings and bracelets, watches from Movado and Rolex, and even items from Tiffany, complete with blue box. They also have cameras, coins, sculptures, and paintings. So how do they compete? With price. The store sources items from estate sales, personal sales, and of course, loan defaults. Baubles at Santa Monica Jewelry and Loan cost a fraction of what they would at the mall. Nineteenth-century oil paintings that sell for between $1,500 and $8,000 at Santa Monica Jewelry and Loan would run you thousands more at a gallery.

So here's the deal: you can browse the fancy shops to get an idea of what sort of bling you're after. Then walk a half block to Santa Monica Jewelry and Loan and pay a lot less. Score!

Address 408 Broadway, Santa Monica, CA 90401, +1 310.451.2840 | Getting there
I-10 to Fifth Street. Metered street parking or city lot. Or by public transit: Big Blue
Bus Route 5 or Route 8. | Hours Mon–Sat 10am–6pm

90__ Santee Alley

A bazaar of bargains

Santee Alley is a bazaar of all the hippest fashion trends, sold at deep discounts. If you're a fan of outlets that borrow from the latest runway styles, like Forever 21 and H&M, you'll love the Alley. The 150 stalls here basically sell the same looks as those brand-name stores – sometimes right down to the fabrics – but you'll generally save a few dollars on each item and even more if you're interested in buying at least three (that's usually where the discounts kick in). The Alley also has all the accessories to complete an outfit: bags, jewelry, makeup, hats, and shoes.

Santee Alley really is an alley, albeit a wide one. It's in downtown's fashion district, located between Santee Street and Maple Avenue; a two-block stretch that runs from Olympic Boulevard to 12th Street. The alley has its origins in the late 1970s when the area's garment wholesalers were struggling to make ends meet. Some of them started opening on the weekends to sell overruns. Reportedly one had the bright idea to put a rack outside his warehouse door. Other wholesalers objected until they saw that his ploy was indeed attracting customers, and they began to follow suit. Soon the alley, previously the domain of delivery trucks, had foot traffic. Another shift happened in the mid to late '80s when wholesalers started pricing for retail shoppers who had previously only been allowed to shop the alley on Saturdays.

These days Santee Alley is open 365 days to wholesalers (usually small shop owners who come to buy in bulk) and bargain hunters alike. There's a classic marketplace atmosphere, with vendors calling out to solicit shoppers and the ritual of haggling in full force.

One thing you're not likely to find here, though, is merchandise from those luxury designers who inspire the trends. So don't get too excited if you see brands like Coach, Michael Kors, and Tory Burch – they are almost sure to be knockoffs.

Address 210 E Olympic Boulevard, Suite 202, Los Angeles, CA 90015 +1 310.203.0101 |
Getting there I-10W to Los Angeles Street or Maple Avenue. Street parking. | **Hours**
Daily 9:30am–6pm, including holidays

91 __ Sara's Lingerie
Underwear that's fit to be seen

Full disclosure: there is a chance you may encounter some suspiciously well-endowed clientele here. Yes, they are porn stars. But the fact that they endorse this store is the reason why you should too. Sara's specializes in stunning lingerie that is custom-fit to enhance each customer's unique curves.

The philosophy at Sara's is that underwear makes the outfit. Mother-and-daughter team Sara Sanfir and Rebecca Krihali stock only the finest quality bras, panties, and corsets, mostly from European houses. They then alter each garment to fit the client. And while many of their regulars are professionals – they also frequently work with celebrities who need to strip down on TV's sexiest shows, or keep everything in place on the red carpet – the store aims to cater to every woman. So whether it's your first bra (Sara's happily welcomes tweens) or your hundredth, they act as if *this* is the bra that could change your life. And it just might.

Sara's carries bras in sizes from 32A to 48H and will order larger if needed. The store sells famous brands like La Perla as well as trending brands like Hanky Panky, which claims to make the world's most comfortable thong, and Underwriters, which only uses natural fibers. Sanfir also aims to serve clients with special needs. So Sara's offers beautiful design solutions for women who have had mastectomies, with padding that can be removed; or if you're a new mother who still wants to feel sexy, they'll turn your favorite silky find into a nursing bra. And if you've recently had liposuction (de rigueur in some circles in L.A.), Sara's also sells compression garments.

While Sara's is known for custom fit, it's also possible to buy right off the rack. Price points begin at about $50 and can run as high as $900. Another bonus: the store officially offers a one-year warranty – if the garment stretches within that time frame, they will re-alter it for free.

Address 12244 Ventura Boulevard, Studio City, CA 91604, +1 818.736.8332, www.saraslingerie.com, info@saraslingerie.com | **Getting there** US-101 to Laurel Canyon Boulevard. Metered street parking. | **Hours** Mon–Sat 10am–6pm, Sun 11am–4pm

92__ Savannah
The greatest hits

Montana Avenue is like the sensible Aunt among Los Angeles shopping haunts. While the others care about being eclectic and cutting edge, her tastes are rooted in the classics. It's not that she's outdated; she just has her own standards. A sure bet for quality merchandise that's fashion forward but doesn't scream, "look at me," Montana offers a mix of unique boutiques, mini-chains, and global brands.

The strip boasts shops like Moondance Jewelry, which sells feminine designs; Kiehl's, the skin-care line that dates back to the 19th century; and Caffe Luxxe, an artisanal coffee shop that roasts its own blends and is known for a traditional European approach. But when it comes to couture, Savannah is the standard-bearer.

Since opening in 1985, Savannah has been stocking the proven designers of the day, such as Dries Van Noten, Stella McCartney, Peter Cohen, Lanvin, Marni, Celine, and The Row, to name a few. Owned by Susan Stone, it is reportedly one of the most successful boutiques in the country.

The store is spacious and the list of designers represented is lengthy, practically guaranteeing something for every taste and type. And with hats, shoes, jewelry, and other accessories, it's a one-stop shop for its regulars. Stone makes seasonal buying trips to Paris, and her clients – who, according to the *New York Times*, span generations – trust she will bring back the greatest hits. Savannah is also known for its trunk shows and the kind of customer service that moneyed patrons are accustomed to: styling advice, clothing loans, and custom ordering.

Montana Avenue is the main drag of northern Santa Monica, considered the conservative half of the beachside town. While tourists and other visitors generally flood the Santa Monica pier and points farther south, the neighborhood surrounding Montana is known as a haven for locals.

Address 706 Montana Avenue, Santa Monica, CA 90403, +1 310.458.2095,
www.savannahsantamonica.com | Getting there I-10 to Lincoln Boulevard or
Fourth Street. Parking behind the store or metered street parking. Or by public transit:
Big Blue Bus Route 3 or 3M. | Hours Mon–Sat 10am–6pm

93_ Sci-Arc Art Supply Store
The raw materials for a growing city

The Southern California Institute of Architecture, known as SCI-Arc, is widely considered to be among the top ten architecture schools in the world. It is known for experimental design, so even its own building is a renegade. The school occupies a 100-year-old freight-yard depot in an industrial section of Los Angeles that was a longtime outpost for artists but has been rapidly gentrifying of late.

SCI-Arc is still very young, having only been around since the early '70s, occupying various locations throughout the years. Although it has called the freight depot home for more than a decade, the institute only put down permanent roots in 2011, when it bought the building. A year later, the SCI-Arc Supply Store opened as a convenience for its 500 students. But local artists soon started frequenting the shop, too. Realizing it was filling a void in the neighborhood, the SCI-Arc Supply Store soon repositioned itself as a community resource – a one-stop shop for art materials.

Not surprisingly, it carries a large selection of building materials, from foam core and museum board to hardwood. Where most art stores offer two or three kinds of sketch pads, SCI-Arc Supply has ten. The selection of drawing pens and color pencils is also extensive. The store tries to stock anything that students recommend, so if the budding architects start asking for a new brand of spray paint for use in model design it will quickly find its way to a shelf. The store also carries books from the school's SCI-Arc Press and is an outpost for Hennessey + Ingalls , a bookstore that specializes in design, art, and architecture.

SCI-Arc is an open campus, so after visiting the store, check out its art gallery, which exhibits experimental works from contemporary architects, or its Kappe Library, which boasts the biggest collection of architecture books in L.A. and defunct design magazines you won't find anywhere else.

Address 960 E Third Street, Los Angeles, CA 90013, +1 213.613.2200, www.sciarc.edu, sciarcsupply@sciarc.edu | Getting there US-101 or I-10 to Alameda Street. Street parking. | Hours Mon–Thurs 10am–6pm, Fri 10am–5pm, Sun–Sat 12pm–5pm

94__Self Edge

A long way from 501s

Selvedge denim is made using shuttle looms, an old-school type of weaving that produces a uniform texture and thickness and a distinctive finished edge. Cheaper, more modern techniques can be used these days, but the quality is less predictable. No wonder then, that the world's best denim brands use the selvedge method.

These are the types of jeans you'll find at Self Edge. Shopping here is an education in denim production, design, and styling. You'll learn, for instance, that unsanforized (or raw denim) – i.e., denim that hasn't been preshrunk or stretched – is best. As such, you should only wash raw denim jeans every four to six weeks to avoid over-shrinking. Even the name of the store is a play on authenticity. Selvedge denim was originally called "self edge."

Self Edge carries denim for both men and women and sizing is determined by waist and length measurements. Many locals consider this to be the city's best jeans store. That's no small accolade since Los Angeles is the Land o' Denim. Movie stars like John Wayne, James Dean, and Marilyn Monroe helped make blue jeans cool and popular with the masses, and they continue to be the Hollywood uniform. Popular brands like 7 for All Mankind, Paige, and True Religion all started here.

Self Edge carries many styles that either hail from or are sourced from Japan, where aficionados believe the best quality unsanforized selvedge is being made these days. They include those by Stevenson Overall Company, Iron Heart, The Flat Head, and Sugar Cane and Co. But you'll also find domestic lines such as Roy by Roy Slaper, a California designer who is obsessed with old denim machines, as well as custom varsity jackets from legendary Portland-based Dehen.

An education in denim at Self Edge doesn't come cheap – it will cost between $200 to $500 to walk out with a rad pair of jeans – but it's certainly Ivy League.

Address 144 N La Brea Avenue, Los Angeles, CA 90036, +1 323.933.9000, www.selfedge.com, denim@selfedge.com | Getting there I-10 to La Brea Avenue. Street parking or a private lot a half block away. | Hours Mon–Sat 12pm–7pm, Sun 12pm–5pm

95 Sewing Arts Center
Where crafty people congregate

It's tricky to ascribe to this shop just one personality, and you should resist the urge to judge it on sight. The main room looks like it would be a haven for grandmas. All the accouterments for creating lovely handmade garments are arranged just so. Threads, trimmings, and other fancies ring a small checkout area. A sea of sewing machines – from standard white to a green flowered Hello Kitty model – are surrounded by bright bolts of materials. Truth be told, a sew-happy grandma would feel right at home here. But then you take a peek behind the walls and realize that so would her punk-rock granddaughter.

Sewing Arts Center is dedicated to making sure that even in a world defined by the ubiquity of "Made in China" labels, there's still a place where anyone can learn how to make a beautiful quilt. Or slacks, or a bag, or metal-studded motorcycle boots.

Sewing Arts also offers tailoring services, but its classes are the heart of the business. Dozens are held each month in the shop's two bright, spacious back rooms, organized based on skill level or necessary time commitment. Take an à la carte class to learn how to make one specific item within a couple hours, a morning, or a day; or spend several weeks working with an expert tailor, learning how to execute perfect hems, skirts, and jackets. It's hard to overemphasize the breadth of the class offerings, some of which really get into the nitty-gritty, like cutting stretch materials, mastering stack-and-whack quilt piecing, or using leatherwork tools.

Russell Conte, a former dancer and costume designer, bought the shop from the original owners in 2000. By then he had been a customer for several years, having discovered it when he needed a machine that could make precise buttonholes. With perfect posture and a kind voice, and wearing impeccably tailored ensembles, Conte makes sure that everyone who walks in the door feels right at home.

Address 3330 Pico Boulevard, Santa Monica, CA 90405, +1 310.450.4300,
www.sewingartscenter.com | Getting there I-10 to Centinela Avenue or Bundy
Drive. Private parking lot. Or by public transit: Big Blue Bus Route 7 to 33rd Street. |
Hours Mon–Thurs 10am–6:30pm, Fri–Sun 10am–5pm

96_ Shareen

The house of reinvention

Going to Shareen Vintage is like going on a treasure hunt. The store is located in a massive unmarked warehouse in what looks like an abandoned part of Los Angeles, a no-man's-land that cars quickly zip through on their way somewhere else. To know you've arrived, keep your eyes out for the brightly colored tutus the staff puts out front as a sign of life.

Once inside, you'll be transported into a girly girl's dream, surrounded by a sea of dresses organized by decade: overly sequined gowns from the *Dallas* '80s, drop-waisted 1920s flapper frocks, and everything in between. Owner Shareen Mitchell and her staff will quickly organize a rack of clothes for you to try on right there in the aisle because there are no dressing rooms (which is why a sign near the door reads "No Boys Allowed"). And you'll likely walk out with an armful of finds. Except for her custom-made lines, which sell for thousands of dollars (her bridal dresses have quickly gained a following), the garments are priced from $50 to $500.

Mitchell founded the business during one of the toughest times in her life. After holding jobs at *Mademoiselle* and *Vogue*, she had embarked on an acting career that seemed to be taking off (she starred as Tony Danza's ex-wife in the short-lived TV series, *Hudson Street*). But by 2004, she'd been hit by the one-two punch of a bad economy and the reality-TV boom it inspired (it costs a lot less for the networks to keep up with the Kardashians than it does to bankroll a scripted dramatic series or sitcom). Broke and in debt she returned to her first love – fashion. Shareen's designs consisted of feminine vintage dresses that she reworked by shortening hemlines, removing sleeves, or refitting bodices. Soon, "It" girls were flocking to her booth at the Melrose Trading Post flea market. Eventually she was able to set up shop in a permanent space and the fashionistas followed.

Address 1721 N Spring Street, Los Angeles, CA 90012, +1 323.276.6226, www.shareen.com, contactla@shareen.com | Getting there I-5 to Broadway, CA-110 to Hill Street. Street parking. | Hours Tues–Sat 10am–5pm, Sun 12pm–6pm

97__Slicetruck Pizza
The sum of its ingredients

Slicetruck used to be L.A.'s favorite pizza truck; now it's the city's favorite pizza joint. The business is owned by the Hanley brothers, Chris and David, who grew up in Chicago and later moved to Brooklyn. Living in two cities that loom large in American pizza lore, they ate their fair share of pies. So when they finally made their way west to Los Angeles, the food-truck capital of the world, they thought a pizza truck could be their ticket to living the Hollywood dream. There was only one problem – they didn't know how to make pizza.

They gave it a shot anyway, creating a product that was good enough for snack-obsessed students if not for discerning palates. One rainy day, business bleak, Chris began roasting garlic to try to lure in customers. Rather than waste an ingredient, he decided to use it as a pizza topping. Thus, the "Hot Garlic" slice was born and Slicetruck had its first bona fide hit. Still, as Chris puts it, "It was no fun selling bad pizza," so the brothers spent their nights honing their skills, and after about two years, they came up with a recipe and technique that is decidedly unique and insanely delicious.

Don't come to Slicetruck expecting a taste of Chicago or Brooklyn. This is California, baby, and the Hanleys approach pizza making as if they were casting a blockbuster movie. Each ingredient has to be a superstar. The dough is made from Kamut brand khorasan wheat, an ancient grain about 10,000 years old; organic San Marzano tomatoes constitute the base of the sauce; the pepperoni comes from Italy and is hand cut in-house; the sausage is homemade by Chris himself… you get the picture. It all comes together harmoniously in a pie that's the epitome of California *fresca*.

Whole pies range from 9 to 16 inches, but the favorite among locals is the Grandma Pizza, which is cooked in a square pan with olive oil that lightly fries the crust.

Address 2012 Sawtelle Boulevard, Los Angeles, CA 90025, +1 310.444.9550, www.slicetruck.com, info@slicetruck.com | Getting there I-405 to Santa Monica Boulevard or Olympic Boulevard. Parking lot behind store. | Hours Tues–Fri 4pm–10pm, Sat–Sun 12pm–10pm

98__South Willard

High art that's low key

Have you ever been awestruck by an interesting find at a museum store? You wonder who made the object and why you haven't discovered it before. Then you either snap it up or tell all your friends about it (sometimes both).

This is how you'll feel about practically every item at South Willard. The store is a marriage of high-fashion menswear and high art, but done in a quiet, straightforward way that eschews the noisy hype L.A. is known for. Owner Ryan Conder has a laid-back vibe comes through in the collaborations he forms to produce exclusive goods for South Willard. These include handmade moccasins with Quoddy, an artisan shoemaker based in Maine; Trail Runner sneakers with Walsh, the storied British footwear manufacturer; and down vests and shirts with Seattle-based Crescent Down Works, which are perfect for exploring the outdoors. Conder also stocks brands like Band of Outsiders, Frank Leder, and Shoes Like Pottery, a Japanese company that makes canvas lace-ups with soft rubber soles that have been vulcanized using a kiln (as with pottery). The store was among the first in L.A. to regularly carry Raf Simons, Dries Van Noten, and Jean Touitou's A.P.C., and still showcases notable designers who may not yet have a foothold in the city, like pant-makers Kosuke Harada and Sayoko Noritake, whose unisex designs for their line, called Tuki, draw from Asian and Western influences.

Conder is a superfan of ceramics, so you'll find work here by artists like David Korty, Roger Herman, Peter Shire, and Ruby Neri. The shop also sells notable local artists like Torbjörn Vejvi and Jason Meadows, and Conder hosts opening receptions for new works that are open to the public. The details of such happenings pop up on the South Willard blog, a must-read that's like a best-of-the-web roundup of news, art, and art news (another example of Conder's curating prowess).

Address 8038 W Third Street, Los Angeles, CA 90048, +1 323.653.6153, www.southwillard.com, info@southwillard.com | **Getting there** I-10 to La Cienega Boulevard. Metered street parking. | **Hours** Mon–Sat 12pm–6pm, Sun 12pm–5pm

99___Spragwerks
Real men make jewelry

Rich Sandomeno was a third-generation mechanic. And perhaps because it was in his blood, he was excellent at it. Problem was, Sandomeno didn't really enjoy his inherited profession; he wanted to do something more creative. Eventually he began taking night classes at a visual arts school and that's where he fell in love with jewelry design.

Ironically, the 15 years he spent working on diesel engines provided the inspiration for Sandomeno's line of jewelry – and its name (a sprag is an engine clutch; *werks* is derived from the German word for a manufacturing plant). Sandomeno has been known to mine discarded engine parts for raw materials. He also sells a ring that looks like a 12-point combination wrench, and another that features a miniature supercharger (also known as a blower) set on the band just as a diamond would be. And he has a love of patina that's probably left over from seeing how beautifully heavy-metal machines color with age.

Even his "store" is more a mechanic's workshop than a retail space. Sandomeno has sold at conventions and flea markets, but he couldn't warm to the idea of sitting around waiting for customers to show up. His goods are available for sale at the workshop, and he passes the time in between appointments working on new designs or projects for other artists. He's happy to welcome visitors, but you'll have to call ahead to make sure he's around. The advantage of making this effort is that you might get first dibs on his latest creation before it hits the Spragwerks website, or end up with a custom piece for an insanely reasonable price.

In 2011, Sandomeno was a runner-up on *Project Accessory* (a spin-off of the wildly popular *Project Runway* television series), where contestants have a day or two to conceive and create a winning design. Sandomeno says the show taught him that he should follow through on his many ideas. You definitely need a workshop for that.

Address 2658 Griffith Boulevard #715, Los Angeles, CA, 90039 (mailing), +1
323.653.6153, www.spragwerks.com, info@spragwerks.com | Getting there Call
or email for a workshop appointment and the address.

100 Sprinkles' Cupcake ATM
Dispensing confectionary bliss

Sprinkles in Beverly Hills, the world's first cupcake bakery, is still as popular as ever, and they've got the lines to prove it. In addition to opening an ice-cream parlor right next door, owner Candace Nelson and her partners had another genius idea: a cupcake ATM. Because, let's be honest, cupcake cravings can and do happen at all hours of the day and night. But here's a tip. When it comes to the Sprinkles ATM, the nighttime is the right time.

That's because during the day visiting the Sprinkles ATM will require parking in a city lot (getting a nearby street spot requires an almost impossible amount of good karma), and then standing on an often long line. And because it's truly fun to step up to the screen of the cotton-candy-pink machine to order your gluten-free red velvet cupcake as the catchy *I Love Sprinkles* theme song plays, you might feel inclined to linger a little (it's the world's first cupcake ATM!!). Then you'll feel a dozen or so impatient pairs of eyes boring judgmentally into the back of your head, and you'll be shamed into moving it along.

But at night… the tourists have returned to their hotels, the locals have retreated to their mansions, and the Sprinkles ATM is all yours! The staff stocks it before they leave for the night so your favorite flavor is right at your fingertips. Take all the time you want to peruse the options. You won't even mind paying a dollar more than you would in the store – after all, the meter out front was not only available, but since it's after hours, it was also free! Prolong the pleasure by taking a stroll down Rodeo, cupcake in hand, as you gaze into the beautifully lit up shop windows.

If it all sounds like a dreamy experience, that's because it is. I would even recommend it as a romantic-night capstone. It'll have you singing, "I love Sprinkles, yes I do, yes I do, the best cupcakes in the world." Although if you're on a date, it might be cooler to hum.

101 Strange Invisible Perfumes

The smell of all-natural

Mass-produced perfumes that haven't been endorsed by celebrities (and therefore need a marketing line) tend to trade on names and images that evoke nature. Think flowers, spices, and the fresh outdoors. Fact is, there is nothing natural about department-store scents. Most are merely chemical concoctions.

Perfumer Alexandra Balahoutis is crying foul and taking fragrance formulation back to its roots. Produced using a process that is hundreds of years old, her Strange Invisible Perfumes are 100 percent botanical, made from flowers, seeds, resins, and other plant-derived ingredients; devoid of synthetic aromas or animal essences. The botanicals are extracted through hydro-distillation – a process whereby they are soaked in water then gently heated to separate the oils, which are blended in a base of organic grape-seed alcohol. The perfumes appeal to people who might not usually wear manufactured scents due to fear of allergic reactions or because of olfactory preferences.

Balahoutis named her company from a line in Shakespeare's *Antony and Cleopatra*: "from the barge a strange invisible perfume hits the sense of the adjacent wharf." Her perfumes complement the wearer's own scent and won't overpower or overwhelm, so Balahoutis suggests a generous application. The names and descriptions of these perfumes are enough to set the senses aflutter: Aquarian Rose (rose brightens a warm sea of marjoram and sandalwood); or Fair Verona (jasmine blossoms sparkle with bergamot, grapefruit, sandalwood, and mimosa absolute).

Balahoutis produces her perfume at a lab that, like her store, is located on the main drag of seaside Venice. In this setting her visibly beautiful, all-natural approach to creating captivating scents doesn't seem at all strange.

Address 1138 Abbot Kinney Boulevard, Venice, CA 90291, +1 310.314.1505, www.siperfumes.com, enquiries@siperfumes.com | Getting there I-405 to Venice Boulevard. Street parking. | Hours Mon–Sat 11am–7pm, Sun 12pm–6pm

102_ The Talpa

Mexican food like Grandma makes

There's a wide range of Mexican cuisine in Los Angeles, bookended by the kind of food you eat at the homes of your Mexican friends (tripe soup, called *menudo*, comes to mind) and the celebrity-chef take on Mexican that costs top dollar at well-appointed restaurants (the word "fusion" is usually salient in this scenario). With its brightly colored interior, stained-glass exterior, multi-generational clientele, and the best taco in L.A., the Talpa is definitely home-style food.

The Talpa's tacos aren't thin, delicate crescent pockets. Handmade – they are thick, crunchy, and knobby. Filled with beef, chicken, shrimp, or pork, they are topped with fresh julienned iceberg lettuce, a slice of tomato, and finely shredded *queso*. The salad topping is a refreshing after-bite to the spicy meats and there's usually a little bit left over on the plate to serve as a palate cleanser.

The Talpa has been serving fresh Mexican food since the 1960s, when the original owner, Lupe Munoz, decided to open a restaurant that honored the traditions of his hometown, the city of Jalpa in the state of Zacatecas. Whoever processed his paperwork at city hall mistook his J for a T and the restaurant was instead named Talpa, which happens to be a city in Jalisco that's home of the annual pilgrimage to the altar of La Chaparrita, or Tiny Virgin Mary. Munoz, who thought the mistake was a lucky omen, embraced the name, and a statue of La Chaparrita still sits on a shelf above the bar.

Talpa has all the other greatest hits of a classic Mexican menu: burritos, ceviche, posole, huevos rancheros. Regular patrons usually order large combination plates so that they don't have to choose between one thing and another. If you've got time to stay, try co-owner Eddie Meza's basil margarita (there's no mix involved here; it's all from scratch). But make sure there's a taco on your plate, especially if it's Taco Tuesday.

Address 11751 W Pico Boulevard, Los Angeles, CA 90064, +1 310.478.3353, www.thetalpa.com | Getting there I-10 to Bundy Drive. Private parking behind store. Or by public transit: Big Blue Bus Route 7 to Barrington Avenue. | Hours Sun–Wed 9am–10pm, Thurs–Sat 9am–11pm

103 __ Wacko / Soap Plant

The wackiest place on earth

Usually when businesses dub themselves wacky, surreal, or lowbrow, it feels like a marketing ploy to perpetuate the perception of coolness. At Wacko Soap Plant, descriptors like these are essentially understatements. This is a 6,500-square-foot emporium of crazy. It might not have been where the birth of cool happened, but genuine cool definitely lives here.

The ringmaster of this retail circus is Billy Shire. His aunt co-owned a natural soap and toiletry store in Berkeley, California, called the Body Shop (it's where the international chain got the name and idea, but that's another story). Shire and his brother convinced their mother, Barbara, to start a similar store in Los Angeles, and the Soap Plant was born in 1971.

Shire was then an artist known for making psychedelic leather outfits worn by rock stars like Elton John. He eventually took over the whole operation, adding the Wacko gift shop and La Luz de Jesus, a gallery that represented counterculture artists like Manuel Ocampo, Joe Coleman, and Robert Williams. Featuring post-pop takes on L.A. themes, it occupies a large room behind the store, adding to the madness of the place.

The core of the business is still exquisite soaps and toiletries, which are custom-scented with essential oils, for about a third of what you'd pay for department-store brands. Glycerin bars come in 25 scents. There's also a sea of kitschy toys and collectibles from around the world including Chinese lucky cats, Day of the Dead art, and religious iconography from Mexico, as well as Japanese robots. For a while this was L.A.'s go-to place for hard-to-find black jeans. And if you ever need to recreate a Caribbean or Latin-American grandma's kitchen, they have bolts and bolts of brightly colored oilcloth. Or perhaps you could use a religious-style glass candle featuring Amy Winehouse, Michael Jackson, or Joey Ramone?

Address 4633 Hollywood Boulevard, Los Angeles, CA 90027, +1 323.663.0122,
www.soapplant.com | Getting there US-101 to Hollywood Boulevard. I-10 to Vermont
Avenue. Metered street parking. | Hours Mon–Wed 11am–7pm, Thurs–Sat 11am–9pm,
Sun 12pm–7pm

104_ Wally's

Bottle shop to the stars

Wally's Wine & Spirits started out as a small liquor shop in 1968. Owner Steve Wallace was an early ambassador for California winemakers, such as Robert Mondavi and Charlie Wagner, whose high-quality bottles he stocked in his store, helping to raise their profiles. Over the years, Wally's has evolved into the city's go-to place for a great bottle. When someone in Hollywood makes a life-changing deal and wants to thank all the little people, she'll probably call Wally's and place orders to be delivered all over town (actually, her assistant will place the call). This practice is so pervasive, in fact, that 85 percent of Wally's business is done over the Internet and by phone, and their signature vans are a zippy fixture on L.A. roads.

From one shop, Wally's has expanded into several neatly whitewashed buildings in a row. Next to the main store is the Cheese Box, which sells more than 150 kinds of cheeses as well as charcuterie, sandwiches, and chocolates. Wally's also has a refrigerated storage house where bottles from world-class wineries are stacked high and rare vintages are kept out of view. Wally's Auctions is responsible for selling off blockbuster consignments, like the 100,000-bottle collection of New York restaurant entrepreneur Roy Welland, worth at least $15 million at acquisition.

Just about everyone who works at Wally's is a wine geek. Christian Navarro, who started as a cashier more than 20 years ago, became Wallace's business partner and is known around town as the wine advisor to the stars. When Wallace retired in 2013, Navarro brought in the Marciano brothers, the owners of Guess, Inc., as investors, and they began expanding the business by opening a Wally's restaurant in Beverly Hills, where patrons can choose from among more than 1500 wines, 150 of them by the glass. Best of all, the restaurant eschews markups. A glass costs exactly what it would if you had bought the bottle at Wally's and poured it at home.

Address 2107 Westwood Boulevard, Los Angeles, CA 90025, +1 310.475.0606, www.wallywine.com, customerservice@wallywine.com | **Getting there** I-10 to Overland Avenue or National Boulevard. Private parking lot. | **Hours** Mon–Sat 10am–7:30pm, Sun 10am–6pm

105__ The Well

The happy-hour blowout

The Well positions itself as many things, a clothing store, a gathering place for creative minds, an event space, and a hair salon. The salon aspect is perhaps most alluring because the Well has settled on a concept that caters very well to its downtown location and its millennial clientele: the happy-hour blowout.

Here's how it works. Like every salon in every town, the Well offers a blow-dry that can last for days. Stylists take brushes, hairdryers, and Oribe hair products to frizzy heads and tame them into sleek works of art. That service usually costs at least $50, but Tuesday to Friday between 4pm and 7pm, the Well offers blowouts for $35, along with complimentary drinks. It's like a mini party before you head out for a date or dinner with friends that guarantees you'll arrive looking and feeling your best.

Here's why it's a blockbuster idea. The Well is in a section of downtown Los Angeles that's in the throes of what everyone now refers to as revitalization, since gentrification has become a pejorative that conjures images of displaced locals and impossibly high rents. The Well is surrounded on all sides by new developments, but you're still likely to encounter a homeless man relieving himself in the alley next to the back entrance. This part of downtown is chock-full of twenty- and thirtysomethings who frequently have plans after work and end up dawdling in the office until traffic subsides. Now they can get a happy-hour makeover without even moving their car.

Also available at the Well are cutting-edge clothing and hair-care products, which means you can not only walk out with a new hairstyle, but a new outfit too. A variety of designers are on sale, but a standout is the shop's own line of T-shirts and tank tops that come in black, white, and "oiled." It's another way this concept store takes something standard and adds a brilliant, revitalizing twist.

Address 1006 S Olive Street, Los Angeles, CA 90015, +1 213.550.4448, www.thewell.la, info@thewell.la | **Getting there** I-10 to Grand Avenue. Private parking behind store. | **Hours** Mon–Sat 11am–8pm, Sun 12pm–5pm

106_ Wertz Brothers

Furnishing up at an affordable price

Everyone gets to that point in their adult life where they crave furniture that doesn't come from IKEA. For those who want high-end materials and style but don't have deep pockets, there's Wertz Brothers. Here you'll find secondhand designer furniture, antiques, and collectibles for a fraction of what they would cost new or from a dealer.

The showroom is massive: 55,000 square feet on two floors, with furniture for every room of the house plus the outdoors. It is frequented by everyone from sophisticated college students to designers on the prowl for something special for their millionaire clients. The business is a member of the American Society of Interior Designers and the Set Decorators Society of America, so co-members of both organizations are frequent shoppers. You never know – you might be getting the opinion of a professional if you ask your fellow browser for some advice.

While the store is called Wertz Brothers, it's currently run by two Wertz cousins, Michael and Ryan, whose fathers, Mike and Larry Jr., purchased it from their father. The store was founded by Michael and Ryan's great-grandfather, Robert Wertz, in 1931.

Secondhand furniture shops in L.A. seem to cater to specific time periods or styles, but Wertz Brothers has items for every taste. Probably because the store sources from individual private sellers. It will send buyers to homes to bid on complete estates or will happily purchase just one special piece after an email connect, followed by closer inspection at the store. Prices also cover a wide range, and no one gets preferential treatment. As their pricing policy reads "Wertz Brothers sells to dealers, decorators, movie studios, foreign buyers, and individuals for the same price. We Do Not Discount! PLEASE DO NOT ASK!"

In a town where VIPs rule the roost, it's nice to find some egalitarianism. Even if you're only on the hunt for a comfortable armchair.

Address 11879 Santa Monica Boulevard, West Los Angeles, CA 90025, +1 310.477.4251, www.wertzbrothers.com, buyers@wertzbrothers.com | **Getting there** I-405 to Santa Monica Boulevard. Private parking lot. | **Hours** Mon–Fri 10am–6pm, Sat 9am–5pm

107__West Coast Classics

Baby, let's cruise

We Angelenos love our wheels. But the classic car collectors among us downright revere theirs. In any given week, it wouldn't be too hard to find a 1950s car show in a diner parking lot; a '70s Mopar car club gathering; or a cruise-night event that brings everyone together. Classic cars are like a religion here, where worship services are always in session. And the culture explains why Hollywood dependably casts vintage models in modern movies, like Clint Eastwood's *Gran Torino*, in which he costars with a 1972 classic Ford.

It helps that L.A.'s climate is perfectly suited for the classics. The warm, dry weather means that cars don't rust practically brand those exposed to East Coast winters or Northwest rainfall. A Southern California car could be many decades old and still look like new. That's why serious collectors from around the world call Peter Doody at West Coast Classics when they are looking for something truly special.

Doody works with car valuation guides spread out around him; he is constantly on the phone discussing auto specs, negotiating prices with people who want to sell him their cars, and with those looking to buy. On any given day, Doody usually has about 30 to 35 vehicles for sale, from a variety of manufacturers and eras. Porsche, Mercedes Benz, and Rolls Royce are usually in the lineup as well as American makers like Cadillac, Ford, and Chevrolet. The cars aren't always in mint condition but they all have something special going for them, and collectors will spend as much as $100,000 to drive one home or have Doody ship it to them.

West Coast Classics is also popular with enthusiasts who just like to scope out what's available and will wander the lot for hours admiring the goods. It's kind of like the experience a music lover might have if he lands at a great festival where all his favorite bands are performing. There's nothing like seeing it live.

Address 1918 Lincoln Boulevard, Santa Monica, CA 90405, +1 310.399.3990, www.thewestcoastclassics.com | **Getting there** I-10 West to Lincoln Boulevard. Street parking. Or by public transit: Big Blue Bus Route 3 to Pico/Lincoln Boulevards. | **Hours** Mon–Fri 9am–5pm, Sat–Sun 11am–5pm

108_ The Whole 9 Gallery

Give peace a chance

Lisa Schultz worked as a marketing executive who specialized in creating massive branding events for multinational corporations and nonprofits. No wonder then, that when she decided to do something purposeful, she took on the biggest issue of all: world peace.

To be clear, Schultz doesn't think she can end wars, or inequality, or even discord in Congress. Her mission is simply to help people in need. Schultz's Whole 9 Gallery sells fine art (they present about six to eight artists each year); jewelry (exquisite pieces like tribal silver earrings from Indonesia and hand-cast pendant necklaces); and items they categorize as "functional art" (artisan-made accessories like vases, key chains, and toys). And 25 percent of everything sold at Whole 9 supports the Peace Project, a nonprofit Schultz created to do good in the world.

Since 2010 the Peace Project has distributed some 10,000 pairs of crutches to amputees in Sierra Leone, even developing its own durable crutch tip that lasts longer in the country's rugged terrain (a peace sign embossed in the rubber leaves an imprint in the user's wake); built dozens of houses for a community on Bantayan Island in the Philippines, where homes were destroyed by 2013's devastating Typhoon Haiyan; and sponsored traveling exhibitions to which artists contribute original pieces on a theme related to peace. The Whole 9 also sells works from the exhibition, which are printed on square wood panels, for $100 each. Every dollar from those sales goes toward the nonprofit work, which includes adding a multipurpose "peace center" – part community market, part community center – to the Filipino housing development.

The Whole 9 Gallery is located in the heart of downtown Culver City. There's a lot of other great shopping and restaurants just steps away, but if you're truly moved to try to do some good, your dollar will go far here.

Address 3830 Main Street, Culver City, CA 90232, +1 310.836.4600,
www.thewhole9.com | Getting there I-10 to Robertson Boulevard. Street parking
or city parking lot. | Hours Mon–Fri 10am–6:30pm, Sat 12pm–6pm

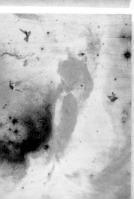

109__Wild Style
Where the cool kids go

Remember Karl Kani – one of the hottest brands of the '90s, known as the favorite designer of rising, hip-hop powerhouses like TuPac and Snoop Dogg? His popularity took a hit as other brands quickly crowded the "urban fashion" space and fickle fashionistas moved on. But when he recently came out with some banging new looks that he hoped would inspire the next generation of street-smart fashion, where did he go to start his comeback? Wild Style, of course.

The easy description of this store is that it gleefully lives up to its name. Wallflowers need not take the walk down its flamboyant entrance ramp flanked by fake palm trees covered in LED lights. Wild Style caters to customers who want to command attention when they enter a room. Think of this as the place where the as-cool entourage of a famously fearless fashionista (Rihanna comes to mind) might come to snatch up some rocking outfits of their own.

This is the home of Walter Van Beirendonck, the most far-out designer among the Antwerp Six, the Belgians who took the fashion world by storm in the late '80s. You'll also find audacious new brands like London-based designers Ashley Williams, known for bold, offbeat prints; Alex Mattsson, whose lines are influenced by biker culture and science fiction; and Nasir Mazhar, who made a name with his "bully cap," which boasts a built-in pencil holder. Wild Style also carries those high-low partnerships that always make fashion news, such as Rick Owens and Raf Simons' collaborations with Adidas, each completely different and madly cool.

The Karl Kani brand relaunched at the store in December 2014 with a party that featured performances by DJ Mustard and underground L.A. rap crew Overdoz, acts that are famous to those in the know. The T-shirts and sweatshirts bearing the brand's signature logo were a throwback as well as something new, and the items sold like wildfire.

Address 7703 Melrose Avenue, Los Angeles, CA 90046, +1 323.651.1223, www.wildstylela.com, info@wildstylela.com | Getting there I-10 to Fairfax Avenue. Metered street parking. | Hours Mon–Sat 12pm–8pm, Sun 12pm–7pm

110__Wing Wa Hing
The good-luck shop

Westerners tend to believe that luck is random and beyond their control, requiring the beneficiary to be in the right place at the right time. Chinese believe there is a lot you can do to influence the potential good fortune of a place, from *feng shui*, the ancient practice of using architectural details to harmonize a living space, to displaying lucky symbols featuring specific colors, numbers, and animals.

Wing Wa Hing is a celebration of these traditions. The store is first and foremost a feast for the eyes – aisle upon aisle of pristinely arranged, tightly packed Chinese objects and knickknacks, many of which carry great cultural significance. For one thing, it's awash in red, the Chinese color for joy and good fortune. There are lucky coins and amulets and a sea of cats in all sizes. The *maneki-neko*, or "beckoning cat," actually originated in Japan but has become a popular fixture in Chinese gift shops, and people buy them to bring positive vibes into their homes and businesses. You'll also find Buddhas, statues of dragons – the mythical animal used to symbolize Chinese culture – and a variety of gifts decorated with knotted cords and tassels, all believed to attract fortuity. The shop is staffed by enthusiastic, helpful attendants who are happy to explain the symbolism of the items.

Any visit to Chinatown should end with a souvenir from Wing Wa Hing, which is just a few storefronts down from the old square that comes alive during celebrations for Chinese New Year. The bright red displays will instantly put you in a good mood. There are gazillions of items that cost just two or three dollars, from chopsticks to bracelets to bright paper lanterns. But it's probably wise to use the opportunity to pick out something more auspicious. Perhaps carvings of the three *feng shui* star gods – Fuk, Luk, and Sau – who bring wealth, happiness, and longevity, the essential human aspirations.

Address 811 N Broadway, Los Angeles, CA 90012, +1 213.437.0710, www.wingwahing.com, wingwahing811@yahoo.com | Getting there I-110 to Hill Street. Metered street parking. | **Hours** Daily 9:30am–6:30pm

111 ZJ Boarding House
Living the California dream

Learning to surf or skate (or both) is at the very least a coming-of-age tradition for many Californians. And for some, the dream never ends. ZJ Boarding House has gear for boarding fans from 2 to 102.

It's hard to believe, but boarding stores are becoming a rarity in L.A. Mostly because the lifestyle has gone mainstream enough that the chains, and even big box stores, generally stock the gear. Going to Costco? Pick up a surfboard with your gallon of ketchup.

ZJ competes by offering something that's hard to replicate: authenticity. Just about everyone who works at the store puts in significant hours on the water and/or concrete. That 16-year-old sales kid probably rode in on the board he's recommending, and the thirtysomething dude ringing up your wetsuit hits the waves at sunup and at midnight.

In addition to big names like Billabong and Quiksilver, ZJ stocks its shelves with smaller, up-and-coming brands, such as Girl and Chocolate Skateboards, Firewire Eco Surfboards, and clothing from Salty Crew and Freedom Artists, a Malibu collective that makes T-shirts emblazoned with original art.

Co-owners Mikke Pierson and Todd Roberts met in the late '80s while volunteering to teach blind and visually impaired kids to surf. At the time, Mikke was affiliated with Zuma Jay Surfboards, Malibu's oldest surf shop, and so ZJ was originally conceived as a satellite when it opened in 1988. While building the business, Todd lived in the store and Mikke in an RV (is there anything more surfer-cool than that!?).

Ironically ZJ split from Zuma Jay's because they wanted to also carry snowboarding gear, but they have since abandoned that business – the market was simply too saturated, and it wasn't worth the headache. Besides, you have to leave the sun and sand to snowboard, and ZJ is all about Santa Monica Beach, which is only a couple blocks away.

Address 2619 Main Street, Santa Monica, CA 90405, +1 310.392.5646, www.zjboardinghouse.com, info@zjbh.com | Getting there I-10 to Fourth Street. Metered street parking. | Hours Mon–Sat 10am–7pm, Sun 10am–6pm

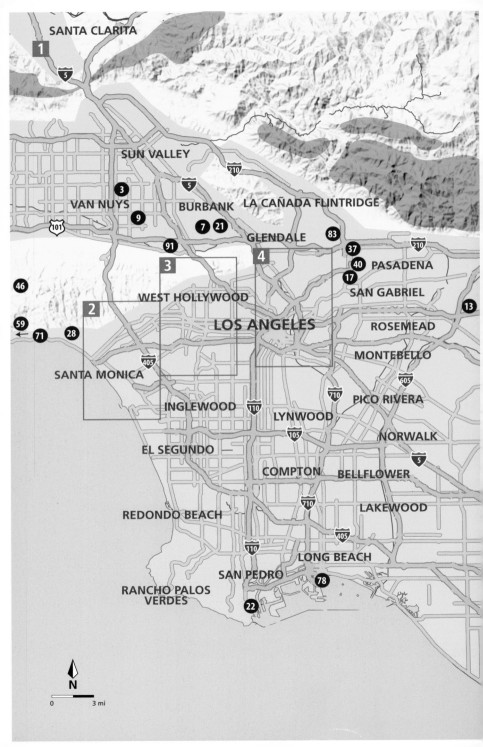

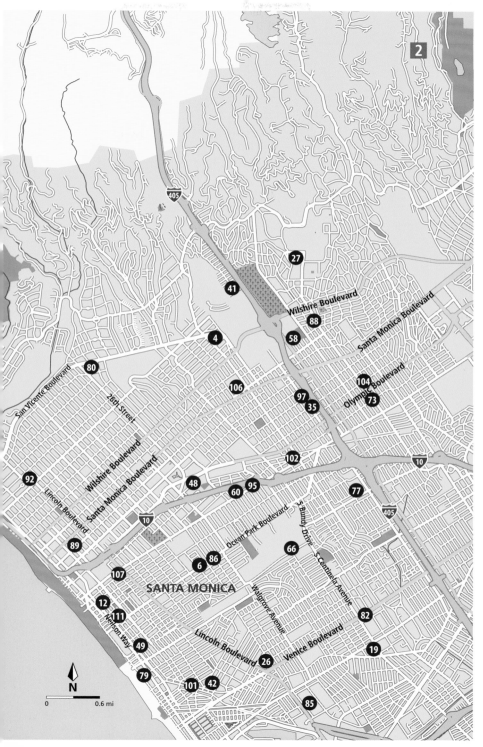

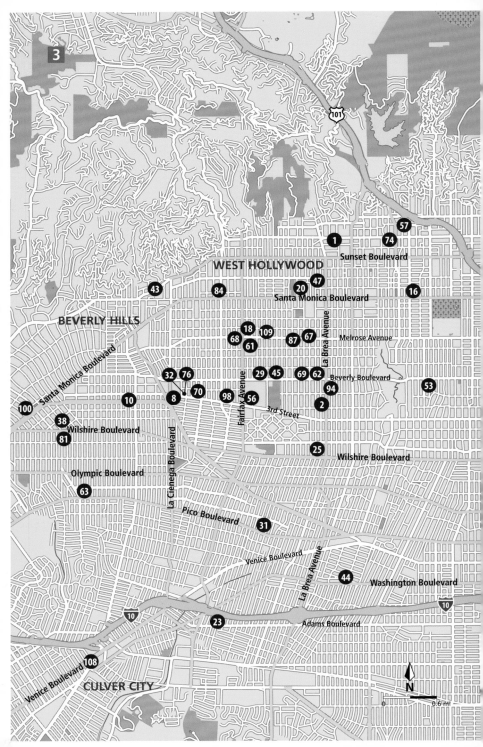

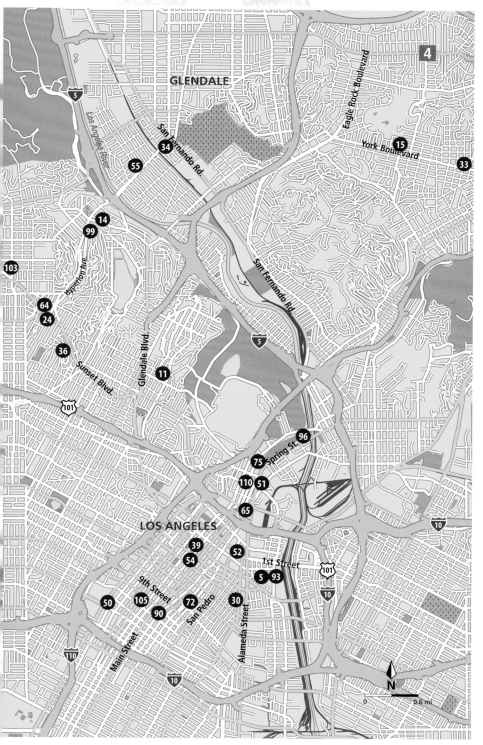

Kirstin von Glasow
**111 SHOPS IN LONDON
THAT YOU SHOULDN'T MISS**
ISBN 978-3-95451-341-3

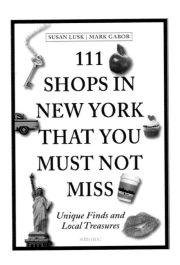

Mark Gabor, Susan Lusk
**111 SHOPS IN NEW YORK
THAT YOU MUST NOT MISS**
ISBN 978-3-95451-351-2

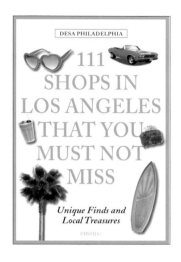

Desa Philadelphia
111 SHOPS IN LOS ANGELES
THAT YOU MUST NOT MISS
ISBN 978-3-95451-615-5

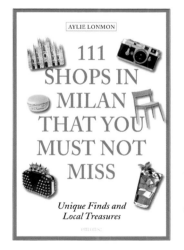

Cristina Morini
111 SHOPS IN MILAN
THAT YOU MUST NOT MISS
ISBN 978-3-95451-637-7

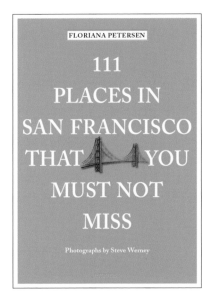

FLORIANA PETERSEN

111

PLACES IN
SAN FRANCISCO
THAT YOU
MUST NOT
MISS

Photographs by Steve Werney

Floriana Petersen
111 PLACES IN SAN FRANCISCO
THAT YOU MUST NOT MISS
ISBN 978-3-95451-609-4

Where can you always find a patch of fog, even on the
sunniest day of the year? What Beaux Arts town house
once belonged to the city's most notorious madam?
Which lighthouse overlooks an underwater graveyard?
And where can you meet a wild flock of parrots in the
midst of the city?

Go off the beaten path to experience 111 fun and
fascinating places in San Francisco that will delight
locals and visitors alike.

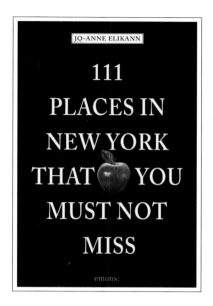

Jo-Anne Elikann
111 PLACES IN NEW YORK
THAT YOU MUST NOT MISS
ISBN 978-3-95451-052-8

Which hot dog joint's phone booth is actually a secret door to a speakeasy? Where is the ATM that dispenses cupcakes instead of cash? And where can you 'fly though the air with the greatest of ease' and view the Freedom Tower?

111 under-the-radar destinations, most of them so unusual, unexpected, or quirky they will astound even seasoned New Yorkers who thought they knew it all!

Acknowledgments

Thank you to all the shop owners and their staff who shared their passion projects with me. Thanks also to Katherine Vu for editorial support and encouragement.

Photo Credits

Photos by Lyudmila Zotova, except: Elyse Walker (p. 64) by Jana Williams Photography; Aldik Home (p. 14), Big Kid (p. 26), Diddy Riese (p. 62), Grist & Toll (p. 88), Louise Green (p. 124), Museum of Flying (p. 140), Rastawear Collection (p. 166), Sara's Lingerie (p. 119), Sewing Arts Center (p. 198), and the Whole 9 Gallery (p. 224), all by Desa Philadelphia; and Gold Bug (p. 82), Guild (p. 92), Requisite (p.117), South Willard (p. 204), and Strange Invisible Perfumes (p. 210), all courtesy of the stores.

The Author

Desa Philadelphia is head writer at the USC School of Cinematic Arts. She previously worked as a journalist, in staff positions at *Time* magazine and the *PBS Newshour*, as a contributor to CNN's *Take Five,* and as a freelance writer and commentator. She is a cofounder of Language Fish LLC, which provides communication strategy, and has worked as a consultant for the UN Global Pulse Initiative, which is focused on using big data analysis for social good. She lives in Los Angeles with her husband, Aaron, and daughter Lilly.

The Photographer

Lyudmila Zotova's photographs have been featured in the *Wall Street Journal,* Yahoo News, and Eater. Zotova is an alumnus of The Art Institute of California-Orange County and resides in San Diego, California. www.lyudmilazotova.com